The Revelation of Jesus Christ

Dr Jim Rennie

Edited by Girish Khare
Freehand Artwork Josh Leigh

AI Generation Lisa Rennie

Book Design & Layout

Saurabh Shrivastava

credits

For any further information please address your emails through website.
Original Illustrations by Josh Leigh
Photographs, illustrations and AI creation from contributing artists, Lisa Rennie & InkCraft

All inputs from the author are to the best of the publisher's knowledge original in all aspects.

The ideas and opinions of the writer are not necessarily those of the publisher nor does the publisher vouch for their authenicity. Request for individual declaration may be entertained but on a case by case basis.

InkCraft · India

contents

Dedication... 06

Foreword.. 07

Preface 11

Christ the Head of the Church 22

Christ the Lamb 40

Christ the Great High Priest 66

Christ the Great Prophet............................. 86

Christ the Judge 124

Christ the King of Kings.............................. 154

Christ Immanuel.. 180

Epilogue 206

All images are representative and do not purport to be the actual images of the deity of Christ or any other person/s being discussed in this book.

Dr Jim Rennie
Youtube: @drjimrennie
website: www.pursuingwisdom.com

Dr Jim Rennie is a devout, committed Christian and medical doctor. Shortly after graduating from Medical School, he and his wife Kathy devoted 14 years to serving as medical missionaries in Zambia. Jim possesses an extraordinary ability to elucidate complex Bible teachings and doctrines, a gifted skill he has honed over many decades.

Dedication

God 'rewards those who earnestly seek him.'
Heb. 11:6

The contents of this book I penned 35 years
ago during the final years of my service
as a medical missionary in Zambia, Africa.
Those were days of immense blessing, as
God illuminated His beautiful word in my
heart while I immersed myself in its truths.
Salvation is not a reward but a gift—unearned
and unattainable through our own efforts.
The knowledge of the Holy One is a reward for
those who diligently study His word and live
in obedience to it.

I dedicate this book to the Rewarder of
my soul, who granted me the privilege of
uncovering some of the wonders of the
prophetic word. It is with great joy that I
share these insights in this publication with
all who choose to read it. May your heart be
blessed, may you be rewarded, and may the
Lord be honoured to the praise of His glory.

Dr Jim Rennie

Foreword

Throughout our lives, we encounter a variety of people. Among these are a few individuals who leave a lasting impact, especially during challenging times. We all remember those special people who have stood by us, offering encouragement in diverse ways. Often, it's these individuals who become friends and mentors. God uses such folk to challenge, comfort, and transform us. For me, Dr Jim Rennie has been such a person. Over the years, he has faithfully provided wise counsel, challenging encouragement, and prayerful support which has played a significant role in my journey.

Dr Rennie has dedicated his life to serving the Lord in numerous ways. At the tender age of ten, he accepted Jesus as his Lord and Saviour. By seventeen, he was already preaching. His gift for teaching blossomed in Youth and Christian camp ministries. God then guided him to pursue a career in medicine. After medical school, Dr Rennie and his wife Kathy travelled to Africa in order to serve in the medical mission field. They spent fourteen years in Zambia where he met numerous medical needs while preaching God's Word, supporting youth programs, and raising three children.

It was during those years that Dr Rennie put pen to paper and wrote the first manuscript of the book you hold in your hands. Jim, Kathy and the family eventually returned to their home country, Canada, in 1987. Jim is a devout Christian and has an extraordinary ability to make plain the sometimes- difficult Bible teachings and doctrines. For the last several decades he has been doing just that. He continues to this day operating a counselling practice that focusses on sharing spiritual encouragement, counsel, and prayer support. He has continued to be very active in serving God in many ways, preaching at a number of churches including his home church, teaching weekly Bible classes and serving as an elder/pastor, all for the glory of his Lord and Saviour.

In today's world, many are questioning the current state of affairs. Rapid changes in political, economic, and cultural landscapes create an overwhelming pace that is difficult to manage, leading to a surge in anxiety and fear. Concerns extend beyond the global future to personal futures as well. Individuals search for answers by delving into history and identifying trends, meticulously analysing news articles, and spending countless hours sifting through various news networks and social media platforms. They heed the insights of experts who attempt to interpret current events and forecast future developments. Although many of these experts exude confidence in their predictions, the accuracy of their foresight often unravels within a matter of years, months, or even weeks.

If you're searching for answers to life's questions and are wondering about what the future holds, I strongly recommend reading and studying Dr Rennie's book "THE REVELATION of JESUS." This book contains Dr Rennie's reflections and personal study of The Revelation of Jesus Christ, which is the last book of the Bible. While simply reading through this book would be beneficial, I highly recommend using it as a study tool to delve deeper into God's word.

The book of Revelation reveals God's plan for the future of mankind and the world. It has a unique narrative in that God's plan is told through the person, work, and glory of Jesus Christ. Dr Rennie guides the reader on a logical, progressive, and insightful journey to understand who Jesus Christ is, what He has achieved for all of us, and how He reveals God's incredible plan for the future. The book of Revelation has perplexed and discouraged many a scholar and reader with its complex symbols, imagery and teachings. In fact, it is for this reason many have chosen not to read or study it. However, Dr Rennie's approach to unravelling the book of Revelation is insightful; he utilises all of the Bible as a canvas to paint a recognisable timeline of human history. This approach highlights how God has, is, and will be in control of the world's past, present, and future, including your own.

Jim has a unique manner of explaining all of the symbols, images, and teachings. He takes the reader on a journey through the books of scripture. This he does in order to locate where those very same symbols, images and teachings have already been mentioned. He is a strong proponent of interpreting scripture with scripture. In fact, he uses over 200 Old Testament references and over 250 New Testament references to piece together the meaning of the book of Revelation. His systematic method aids in the thorough study of Revelation, as he leads the reader through the Seven visions of Jesus Christ penned by Apostle John, under the guidance of the Holy Spirit. These visions present the seven ways in which Jesus Christ is recognized: The Head of the Church, The Lamb, The Great High Priest, The Great Prophet, The Judge, The King of Kings, and Immanuel, God with us.

If you seek to understand more about who Jesus Christ is and the future of this world, mankind, and yourself, I highly recommend using Dr Rennie's book. Dedicate yourself to the study of the book of Revelation with prayer and confidence. "Blessed is the one who reads the words of this prophecy, and blessed are those who hear it and take to heart what is written in it, because the time is near" (Revelation 1:3). "Behold, I am coming soon! Blessed is he who keeps the words of the prophecy in this book" (Revelation 22:7).

In His Service
Laurence Wragg

Preface

The Revelation of Jesus Christ (Rev. 1:1)

The testimony of Jesus is the spirit of prophecy (Rev. 19:11)

Over past years I have given the material in this book as a series of Bible talks to various groups. A common reaction of those who heard has been, "This study has helped me put it all together."

As a Christian for many years, I have found great joy in studying God's word. However, I have often struggled with retaining what I learned and connecting different parts of the scriptures. For example, what I was presently learning did not connect with what I had learned before.

Then I began to understand the truth expressed in Revelation 19:11, "The testimony of Jesus is the spirit of prophecy." I believe that this means the witness to Jesus is the great unifying principle that binds all of scripture together into one whole. To find Jesus in various scriptures is to relate them to one another, making them both understandable and memorable.

During my time as an undergraduate, I took various unrelated courses. I often wondered about the relevance of studying English literature when I was also learning about organic chemistry. With no niche for it in my understanding of this scheme of things, it quickly disappeared from my mind.

However, my perspective changed when I started medical school. I realized that every subject was interconnected, all revolving around the human body. Physiology and anatomy, for example, were not isolated but intricately linked to each other. As I studied physiology, I also gained knowledge of anatomy, and everything started to make more sense and became more memorable.

On the day of His resurrection, Jesus approached two of His confused and despondent disciples on the road to Emmaus. Endeavouring to restore their shattered faith, he said to them, "Oh foolish men and slow of heart to believe in all that the prophets have spoken! Was it not necessary for the Christ to suffer these things and to enter His glory?" Then, "beginning with Moses and all the prophets, He explained to them the things concerning Himself in all the Scriptures!" (Luke 24:27). On another occasion, Jesus said to those who opposed Him, "You search the Scriptures because you think that in them you have eternal life; and it is these that bear witness of Me" (John 5:39).

Man's profound desire for order, or a unifying principle, is demonstrated by the tremendous success of the book "A Brief History of Time," which topped the bestseller lists for months. The book was authored by the late Stephen Hawking, a world-renowned physicist. His fundamental assertion is that at the core of all our scientific knowledge lies a grand unifying principle. This principle remains beyond humanity's comprehension but will soon be understood. Regrettably, Hawking did not accept God's testimony regarding His Son, as stated in Colossians 1:17, "In Him all things hold together". (Hawking, who passed away at the age of 76, wrote "There is no God" in his final, posthumous book "Brief Answers to the Big Questions." He also wrote that "no one directs the universe").

The study of Revelation begins with the premise that the primary purpose of prophecy is to reveal Christ. When we look for Him, we will find Him. He won't be a side issue, but rather the great unifying force. He makes the book hold together. Of course, we will also learn details of "the things which must shortly take place" (Rev. 1:1). However, what is going to happen, and, to whom, are of secondary importance. The real purpose is to discover Who is going to make it happen! It has been well said that history (past or future) is HIS STORY. History is only the stage for the magnificent revealing of the glories of the Son of God.

The questions, "What is going to happen?" and "To whom?", have their place. I believe the church will be rescued from this world before the great tribulation recorded in Revelation. I believe that the tribulation is a seven-year period in the future when God will be dealing with Israel and the nations. I believe these events will not have a direct bearing on the church. Even so, I will study Revelation to learn more about the Lord Jesus Christ. If I fail to do so, as is the sad position of many Christians, I will miss a great blessing. The Revelation is, in my estimation, the great culmination and summary of the teaching about Christ in all the Scriptures.

Three Important Connections

1. The Number Seven Connection

Seven is the number of perfection, not only in theology, but in many areas of life. Consider these examples: Seven is an important measure of time - seven days in a week. Seven is a measure of colour - red, orange, yellow, green, blue, indigo, violet are the seven colours of the rainbow. Seven is a measure of music - seven different notes in the scale, with a repetition of the first note to form the octave. Seven is a measure in physiology - the natural

resonance of our bodies is seven cycles per second.
It should not be surprising, then, that God, who created time, music, colour, and our physical bodies, should frequently use this number in His scriptures. The number seven is specifically mentioned 54 times in the book of Revelation, not to mention other occasions when things are grouped into sevens without actually being numbered.

It should also be no surprise, then, that the book may be seen as divided into seven parts. One major vision of Jesus Christ opens each of these sections, seven visions in all. Each picture of Christ presents Him in a different role. This role gives each section of the book its particular character. Christ initiates the events in each section, and thereby controls them throughout.

Viewed in this way, Revelation is not strictly a chronology of events, but rather a montage of scenes with the Lord Jesus as the star in each scene. Like the colours of the rainbow and the notes of the scale, these seven visions of Christ blend together in glorious harmony to offer to us the most complete display of the awesome greatness of Christ in all the Scriptures.

2. The Tabernacle Connection

One of the most intriguing parts of Old Testament history is the account of Moses receiving the law of God on Mount Sinai. However, at the same time Moses was given the Ten Commandments on Mount Sinai, he was also given specific instructions by God to build a tabernacle in the middle of the camp of Israel, a tent of meeting, where God could meet with His people. Virtually every professing Christian knows about the Ten Commandments, but comparatively few know about the tabernacle, or understand the significance of it. Unfortunately, they have missed the best part!

In the gospel of John, the miracle of the incarnation is described this way, "And the Word became flesh, and dwelt among us, and we beheld His glory, glory as of the only begotten of the Father, full of grace and truth" (John 1:14). The word "dwelt" could also be translated "tabernacled", because they mean the same thing. The Ten Commandments was only half the story God gave to Moses, and the worst half at that! The Law told Israel their God was holy and righteous and would therefore judge sinners to the full extent of the Law (Ex. 18:4). The tabernacle was meant to be a picture of Jesus, and, as such conveyed the good news! God has made a way whereby guilty sinners can come to Him, receive forgiveness, and experience the joy and peace of an intimate relationship with their Creator. John 1:17 states, "The Law was given through Moses; grace and truth were realized through Jesus Christ". The good news of God's grace and mercy, pictured in the tabernacle, was fully realized in the coming of Israel's Messiah, our Saviour Jesus Christ.

The permanent place for God's dwelling in Israel was the temple, originally built by King Solomon. The Lord made an interesting connection between Himself and the temple (which by that time was a new temple built by Herod) when He prophesied, "Destroy this temple and in three days I will raise it up"(John 2:19). Because this took place in the temple courts, many thought that He was referring to the temple building, but Jesus was referring to His own body. The Lord invited His listeners to understand the true significance of His presence among them. The temple building, and all the services connected with it, were symbols of the Messiah. The story of the temple reveals that God would come to be physically present with His people in order to bring them back into relationship with Himself. You may ask "What does this have to do with the book of Revelation?". "It has everything to do with it!" On almost every page of Revelation you will find reference to the tabernacle and to its permanent structure, the temple.

In the construction plans given to Moses, God said, "According to all that I am going to show you, as the pattern of the tabernacle and the pattern of all its furniture, just so you shall construct it "(Ex. 25:9). The instructions were explicit because these things were to be an exact replica of a heavenly tabernacle where God lives (Heb 8:5, 9:11).   Just as a human father may decorate his home with remembrances of his son, so the Heavenly Father furnishes heaven with remembrances of His beloved Son.

There were seven articles of furniture in the tabernacle. We will see that they each teach a different truth concerning the Lord Jesus. However, what is most beautiful to behold is that these seven articles of furniture in the tabernacle have their exact counterparts in the seven visions of Christ in the book of Revelation!

3. The Zechariah Connection

"And beginning with Moses and all the prophets He explained to them the things concerning Himself in all the Scriptures"(Luke 24:27). Surely then, He would not disregard one of the last, but far from the least, of the prophets of Israel? In fact, Zechariah is full of references to Christ.

Zechariah begins with a series of eight visions culminating by a symbolic crowning of Joshua, the high priest. We will see that these visions parallel the visions and scenes of Revelation in exact order, with one notable exception. The first three chapters of the book of Revelation are not envisaged in the book of Zechariah. The reason for this omission is easily discovered. The first three chapters of Revelation have to do with the church in this age of grace. The church was a mystery not revealed to the prophets of the Old Testament, as explained in Eph. 3:4-6. Zechariah's visions pick up the action of Revelation beginning in chapter 4, when the church has already been taken to heaven.

As I see the tabernacle teaching and the message of the prophets like Zechariah all meeting together in Revelation, my spirit gives praise to the God of order. Let the physicists write their histories of time. God has already written His own history of time in the Scriptures, both the past and the future, with Jesus as the unifying force who brings it all together. Finding Christ in the Scriptures makes them memorable, magnificent and life-changing!

TABLE:
SEVEN VISIONS OF CHRIST IN REVELATION

Vision of Christ	Section of Book introduced by Christ	Relationship to tabernacle furniture	Relationship to Visions of Zechariah	Application to believers
Head of the Church 1:9-20	Seven letters Ch 1-3	Table of bread	No vision	Fellowship
Lamb of God (Saviour) 5:1-7	Seven seals Ch 4-7	Altar of sacrifice	Visions of 4's & surveyor 1:7-2:13	Worship
High Priest 8:1-5	Seven trumpets Ch 8-9	Golden altar	Vision of Joshua the High Priest 3:1-10	Intercessory prayer
Prophet 10:1-11	Seven persons Ch 10-14:5	Lampstand	Vision of the golden lampstand 4:1-14	Witness
Judge 14:14-16	Seven bowls Ch 14:6-18	Laver (sea in temple)	Vision of the flying scroll and ephah Eph. 5: 1-11	Judgment and cleansing
King of Kings 19:11-16	Seven dooms Ch 19-20	Ark of the Covenant	Vision of 4 chariots 6:1-8	Glory and victory
Immanuel 21:3-7	Seven new things 21-22	Mercy seat	The crowning of Joshua 6:9-15	Life in Heaven

What the tabernacle furniture teaches about Christ

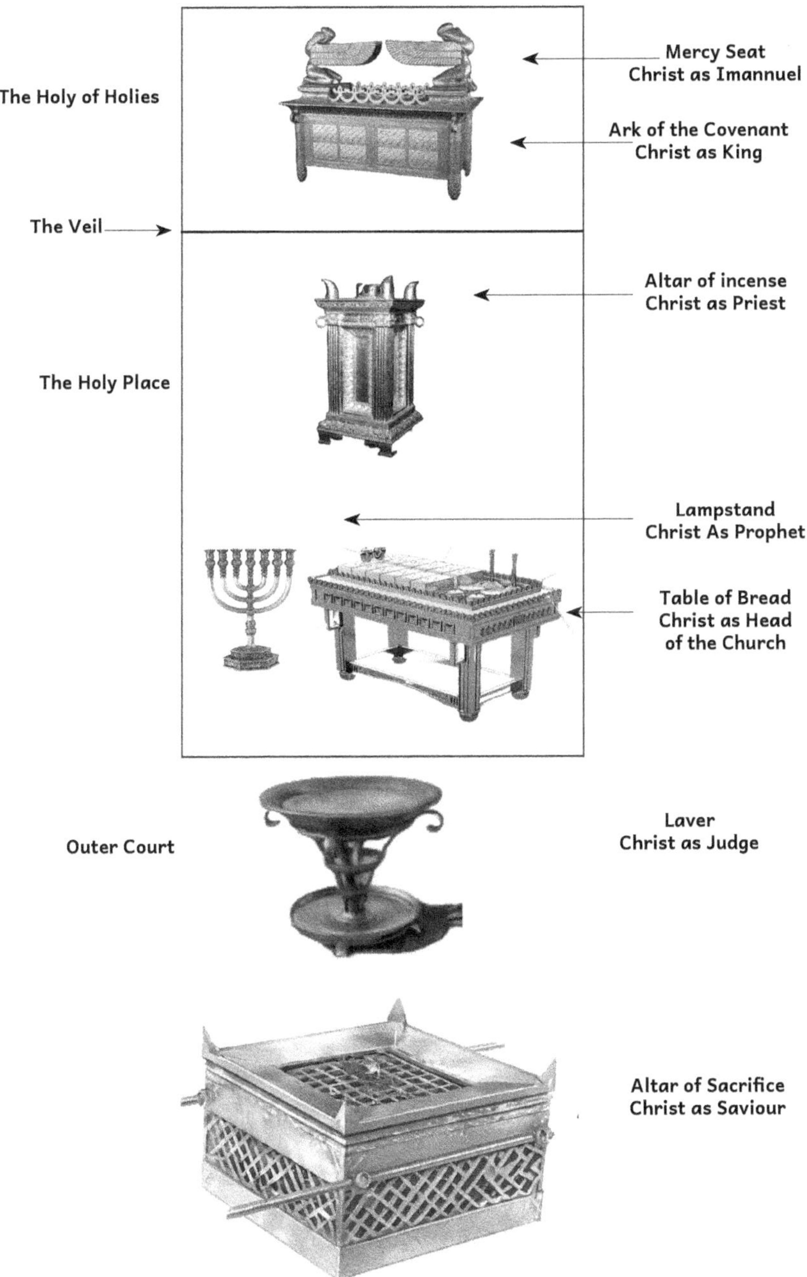

Vision I

CHRIST
THE HEAD OF THE CHURCH

John the apostle
7 Letters to 7 Churches
Ephesus
Smyrna
Pergamum
Thyatira
Sardis
Philadelphia
Laodicea

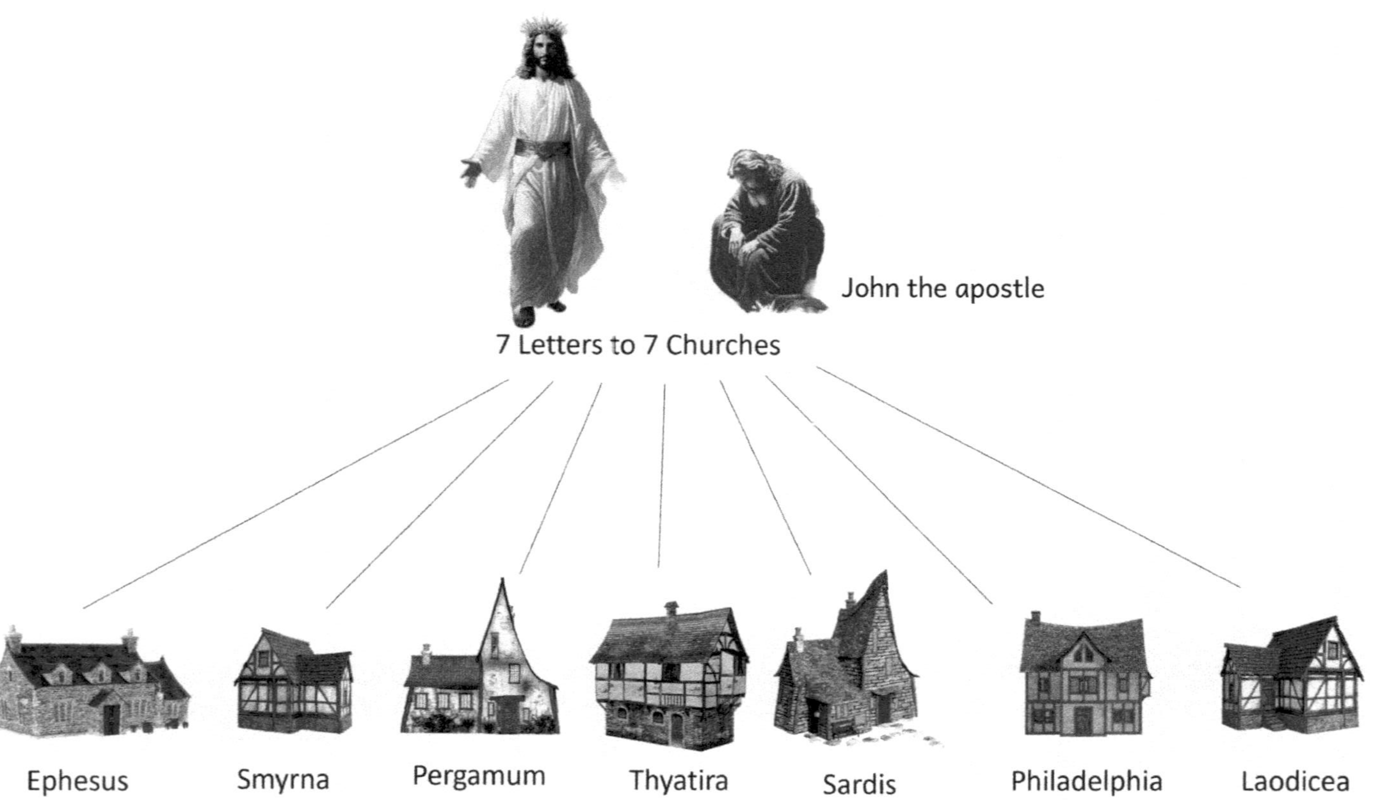

24

Vision I

CHRIST – THE HEAD OF THE CHURCH

The opening scene of Revelation is cast on a desolate island in the Aegean Sea off the coast of Asia Minor. There the aged apostle John is living in exile because of his witness for the Lord Jesus. However, he is not dismayed. Far from it! He is "in the Spirit", enjoying the fellowship of the Lord, on "the Lord's Day". The special day for worship in the early church was the first day of the week, the resurrection day, and John, although deprived of the fellowship of other believers, is nonetheless engaged in communion with Christ. What he is to learn though, is how very close Christ is to him, even in that lonely place. In fact, the Lord is right there! That is what we need to learn also, that the Lord is right there with us as our HEAD. He longs for fellowship with us. He has promised, "Lo, I am with you always ..." (Matt. 28:20).

John hears first a voice behind him, telling him to write in a book what he sees and send it to the seven churches on the mainland of Asia Minor. When he turns to hear who is speaking, he first sees seven golden lampstands. We are told later that the seven lampstands represent the seven churches to which the letters will be sent (Rev. 1:20).

The lampstands are a fitting symbol for the church in the world, because Jesus said to His disciples, "You are the light of the world" (Matt 5:14), the light being a symbol of witness and testimony. However, the church will never shine without the fellowship of her risen Head, so Christ is among the lampstands, showing that the desire of His heart is to be with His church. "Where two or three are gathered together in My Name, there am I in their midst" (Matt. 18:20). His sad cry to the church at Ephesus is, "You have left your first love" (2:4). The inevitable result of continuing on without the loving companionship of the Lord would be disaster. "I will remove your lampstand out of its place" (2:5).

This is the basic message that the Lord seeks to convey. He is the Head of the body, the heavenly Bridegroom, and as such, desires fellowship with individual believers, and with His church. Just as an engaged man would send love letters to his future bride, so the Lord sends these letters … love letters (Rev. 3:9,19) … to His church, to comfort, to encourage, to instruct, and to warn.

A PORTRAIT OF THE LORD

However, as much as John also loves the church, his eyes are not upon the lampstands, but upon the glorious One who stands among them, the Head of the Church. How do we know that this is the Lord? He is not named as such, but He is identified to us by His DESCRIPTION, and His WORDS.

In Psalm 45, the sons of Korah sing a love song describing the magnificent appearance of the Lord and King as He appears to His bride. Here we have the New Testament refrain of that love song, a full description of the Lord in resurrection glory. As we shall see, it is linked with appearances of the Lord in the Old Testament and forms a basis for our recognition of Him further on in Revelation.

HIS DESCRIPTION

1. "One like a son of man" (Rev 1:13)

This phrase comes out of Ezekiel's vision of the glorious throne of God (Ez. 1:26). "On the throne was a figure with the appearance of a man". Again, in Dan. 7:13, "And behold, with the clouds of heaven, One like the Son of man was coming … and to Him was given dominion, glory, and a kingdom…". Jesus said of Himself, "From now on a Son of Man will be seated at the right hand of the power of God" (Luke 22:69). Jesus often referred to Himself by this name. It was at once a statement concerning His full humanity, and a claim to be the One to fill the throne of the universe.

2. "Clothed in a robe reaching to the feet, and girded across His breast with a golden girdle" (Rev 1:13)

This was the uniform of the priest of Israel (Ex. 28: 2-5). We will later see that Christ appears in the office of High Priest in Revelation. A similarly dressed person appeared to Daniel. "Behold, there was a certain man dressed in linen, whose waist was girded with a belt of pure gold of Uphaz" (Dan. 10:5). We take this appearing to be the preincarnate Christ.

3. "His head and His hair were white like wool, like snow" (Rev 1:14)

In Daniel's vision of the court of heaven, the "Ancient of Days", who is the Lord God, appears seated on a throne,where the hair of his head was white like wool (Dan 7:9). Proverbs 16:31 tells us that this signifies the wisdom of righteousness."His name will be called Wonderful Counselor..." (Is. 9:6).

4."His eyes were like a flame of fire" (Rev 1:14)

The fire speaks of judgment, and the eyes of knowledge and insight. David said of the Lord, "His eyes behold, His eyelids test the sons of men" (Ps. 11:4)."And there is no creature hidden from His sight, but all things are open and laid bare before the eyes of Him with whom we have to do" (Heb. 4:13). In the vision of Daniel 10 we read, "His eyes were like flaming torches".

5."His feet were like burnished bronze, when it has been caused to glow in a furnace" (Rev 1:15)

Bronze speaks of strength and the furnace speaks of trials. This symbolizes the kind of strength that is sufficient for every trial. Once again, in the vision of Daniel 10 there is a similar description ... "His arms and feet like the gleam of polished bronze".

6 "His voice was like the sound of many waters" (Rev 1:15)

What a voice it must have been to carry to the ears of over five thousand people gathered on a hillside in Galilee! The Africans first called the mighty Victoria Falls "Mosi au Tunya", which means "The Smoke That Thunders". The voice of the Lord thunders as well. "Truly, truly, I say to you, an hour is coming and now is, when the dead shall hear the voice of the Son of God, and those who hear shall live" (John 5:25). The Lord's voice pierces the graves and wakes the dead!

7. "And in His right hand He held seven stars" (Rev 1:16)
The Lord solves this mystery for us by telling us that "the seven stars are the angels of the seven churches" (Rev. 1:20). If there are guardian angels for children (Matt. 18:10), and angels to represent whole nations (Dan.12:1), then it is reasonable to believe from this that each church has its own angelic representative as well. But the Lord is in control over all. He has them in His right hand.

8. "Out of His mouth came a sharp two-edged sword" (Rev 1:16)

Hebrews 4:12 states, "For the word of God is living and active, and sharper than any two-edged sword, …". This symbolizes the awesome authority and power of the written word. But here we have that same awesome authority from the mouth of the Living Word, Jesus Christ.

9. "His face was like the sun shining in its strength" (Rev 1:16)

When the Lord was seen in glory on the Mount of Transfiguration, it says, "His face shone like the sun" (Matt. 17:2). When Paul describes his sight of the face of Jesus on the Damascus Road, he says, "I saw on the way a light from heaven, brighter than the sun, shining all around me and on those who were journeying with me" (Acts 26:13). Lastly, it must be noted again in the vision of Daniel 10 that there is a corresponding description, "his face had the appearance of lightning". No other has such a face as this majestic One who will one day light up heaven with His presence (Rev. 21:23).

HIS WORDS

When John sees such a glorious person, it is no wonder that he falls at his feet as a dead man. But this One compassionately lays His right hand upon him and says, "Do not be afraid". His further words show who He really is.

1. "I am the first and the last" (Rev 1:17)

Three times in the book of Isaiah, Jehovah uses this name for Himself (Is. 41:4, 44:6, 48:6). This One dares call Himself by a name of Jehovah!

**2.	"And the Living One" (Rev 1:18)**

Twice in the book of Daniel, the Most High is referred to as "Him who lives forever" (Dan 4:34, 12:7). This One dares call Himself by a name of the Most High!
**3.	"And I was dead, and behold, I am alive forever more" (Rev 1:18)**

Wonder of wonders that "the Living One" should say that once He was dead! A similarly paradoxical statement is made by Peter at Pentecost, "You ... put to death the Prince of life ..." (Acts 3:15). But, praise God, he does not end his sermon there. He continues, "whom God raised from the dead". This description fits only one person, the Lord Jesus.

**4.	"And I have the keys of death and of Hades" (Rev 1:18)**

These keys were wrested from "the one who had the power of death, that is, the devil" (Heb. 4:14). By death, Jesus delivered "those who through the fear of death were all their lifetime subject to bondage"(Heb. 2:14 - 25).

By the description and words of this glorious person, He can be none other than the Lord Jesus Christ. He appears as the LORD OF THE CHURCH, the "head of the body" (Col. 1:18). He shows His personal concern for His church by appearing amongst the seven golden candlesticks.

He desires their collective fellowship. "Where two or three are gathered in My Name, there I am in their midst" (Matt. 18:20). He holds the seven stars in His right hand. He is not an absentee landlord, but rather is vitally interested in the spiritual life of the church. He lays His right hand upon John, the right hand being a symbol of fellowship. The Lord is reaching out in love to personally comfort His servant. The messages that follow are communications motivated by love and a desire for fellowship.

Seven Messages from the Lord to the Seven Churches

The Lord Jesus then tells John, "Write therefore the things which you have seen" (that is, the vision of the Lord Jesus in chapter 1), "and the things which are" (that is, the description of the seven churches in chapters 2 and 3), "and the things which shall take place after these things" (that is, the things pertaining to the future, beginning in chapter 4 and on to the end of the book).

These churches were all located in cities in Asia Minor. They were well known to John because he, according to tradition, worked with the churches of Asia Minor for many years. However, the Lord knew them better, and His words of blessing and judgment reveal the true spiritual state of each congregation.

It is of vital importance to note that in each instance

the Lord prefaces His remarks to the churches with a reference to Himself, most of which are a part of the description of the Lord in chapter 1. Each descriptive reference is pertinent to the message spoken to each church. This pattern recurs throughout the book of Revelation and serves as a template for the book! The vision of Christ both initiates and sets the tone for what follows. This further emphasizes the CENTRALITY of Christ.

The following paragraph shows the relationship between the vision of Christ and the main message to each Church.

CHURCH	MAIN MESSAGE	MESSAGE IN VISION OF CHRIST
Ephesus	You have left your first love (2:4)	I want to walk with you and have loving fellowship with you
Smyrna	You will have tribulation (2:10)	Take courage in remembering my victory over death
Pergamum	Some hold false teaching (2: 14-15)	My word will judge between those right and those wrong
Thyatira	They are guilty of immorality (2:20)	I will search your hearts and I will judge the guilty ones
Sardis	You are dead (3:1)	Wake up
Philadelphia	You have kept my word (3:8, 10)	I open to you the door of blessing and privilege
Laodicea	You are wretched, poor, blind, naked (3:17)	Your life should center in Me, the Beginning and the End

The Tabernacle Connection: The table of bread (Rev. 3:20)

Perhaps the best known and most touching of all the verses in Revelation is Rev. 3:20. "Behold, I stand at the door and knock; if anyone hears my voice and opens the door, I will come in to him, and will dine with him, and he with Me."

The eating of food together at a table is a perfect symbol of fellowship. When Jacob and Laban agreed to end their quarrel, they sat down to eat a meal together (Gen. 31:54). When King David wished to honor the memory of his loving friend, Jonathan, he sat Mephibosheth, Jonathan's lone surviving relative, at his table (II Sam. 9:11). David knew well the blessing of sitting at the King's table, for when he was just a shepherd, he wrote, "You prepare a table before me in the presence of my enemies" (Ps. 23:5).

The Lord Jesus often sat at a table in company with others, at least ten times in Luke's gospel alone. He was a "people" person. He loved men's souls, and He showed it by eating with both Pharisee and publican (Luke 7:36, 19:5), as well as preparing a meal for others (John 21:9).

This aspect of Christ's fellowshipping with His church is depicted by the table of bread in the tabernacle. Many will appreciate that the bread upon the table presents Christ as the Bread of Life. But Christ is also the table which holds the bread. As members of Christ, we meet there with Him for fellowship, and we feed upon Him (Heb. 13:10).

Priests at the table

Upon a pure gold table in the Holy Place were 12 loaves of bread. Every Sabbath the priests would enter to remove the old loaves of bread and replace them with fresh loaves. They then took the old loaves of bread and ate them together in a holy place (Lev. 24:5-9). There are several things to note concerning this:

1. There were 12 loaves of bread, one for each of the 12 tribes of Israel. All Israel was represented at this table of fellowship.

2. The bread was called the "Bread of the Presence" (Ex. 25:30). By eating this bread they were enjoying and celebrating the presence of the Lord with them.

3.The priests ate the bread together. It was a communal act. Not only were they enjoying fellowship with God, but they were enjoying fellowship with one another also. "Is not the bread which we break a sharing in the body of Christ? Since there is one bread, we who are many are one body, for we all partake of the one bread" (I Cor. 10:16-17).

4.The priests ate the bread together on a weekly basis. "And on the first day of the week, when we were gathered together to break bread ..." (Acts 20:7). "As often as you eat this bread and drink the cup, you proclaim the Lord's death until He comes" (I Cor. 11:26). As members of the body of Christ, the early church met weekly on the first day of the week to remember the Lord and break bread together (Acts 2:46, 20:7, I Cor. 16:2).

5.The bread was to be eaten in a holy place. Before there can be fellowship with the risen Lord, there must be holiness of life. For, "whoever eats the bread or drinks the cup of the Lord in an unworthy manner, shall be guilty of the body and the blood of the Lord" (I Cor. 11:27). This is stressed in the references to eating which occur in the letters to the churches. Consider two references:

"...you have there some who hold the teaching of Balaam, who kept teaching Balak to put a stumbling block before the sons of Israel, to eat things sacrificed to idols, and to commit acts of immorality" (2:14).

"...she teaches and leads my bondservants astray, so that they commit acts of immorality and eat things sacrificed to idols" (2:20).

In these churches, they were not eating at the table of the Lord, but rather at the table of demons! (I Cor. 10:21). They were partaking in UNHOLY COMMUNION. The door of the church was closed to Christ. The heart's door of many believers is closed to Him also. He, for love and mercy, will not leave them in such a state of spiritual poverty, so discipline is applied to the disobedient ones.

On the other hand, the messages to the overcomers reflect a situation where there is obedience and holiness of life, and a corresponding fellowship with God. Consider these references:

"To him who overcomes I grant to eat of the tree of life, which is in the paradise of God" (2:7).

"To him who overcomes, to him I will give some of the hidden manna…" (2:17)

These believers were enjoying HOLY COMMUNION. Fellowship with the Lord is based on holiness which results from a practical, daily obedience to Christ and a yielding to His lordship. This is the key to victory in the Christian life.

The Zechariah Connection

I have asserted that the visions in the opening chapters of Zechariah correspond with the subject matter of Revelation, but with this notable exception! There is no reference to the Lord of the Church, nor to the symbol of the Table of Bread, in the visions of Zechariah. That is easy to understand, because Paul makes clear that the church was a mystery in the Old Testament, something revealed only in the New Testament (Eph. 3:1-6).

Summary

Jesus appears as the Head of the church. His chief desire is fellowship with His people. That fellowship is symbolized by a table in the key verse of the passage, Rev. 3:20. The Table of Bread in the tabernacle expresses that same desire on God's part to fellowship with His people. The Lord Jesus is that table and that bread. He is the One through whom we have fellowship with God and with each other (I John 1:3).

Vision II

CHRIST

THE LAMB, THE SAVIOUR

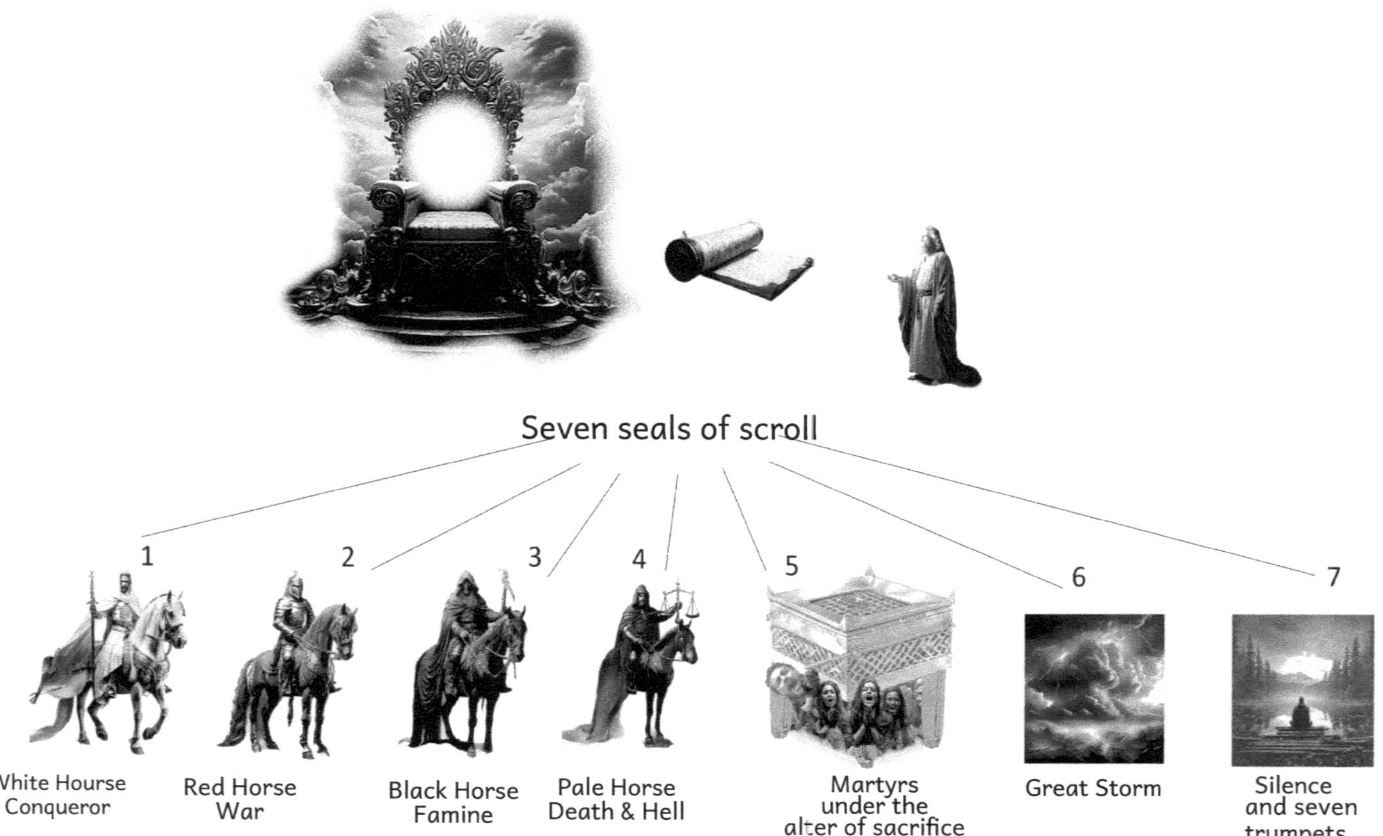

Seven seals of scroll
1
White Hourse
Conqueror
2
Red Horse
War
3
Black Horse
Famine
4
Pale Horse
Death & Hell
5
Martyrs
under the
alter of sacrifice
6
Great Storm
7
Silence
and seven
trumpets

Vision II

Christ the Lamb, the Saviour

"After these things I looked, and behold, a door standing open in heaven, and the first voice which I had heard, like the sound of a trumpet speaking with me, said, "Come up here and I will show you what must take place after these things." (Rev.4:1-2). Although the door to many a believer's life is closed to Christ, as seen in Revelation 3:20, the door to Christ's home is now opened wide to receive a faithful saint.

What a contrast! From a lonely existence on a desolate island, John is now transported into the very throne room of God, the master control room of the universe. John hears a familiar voice, the voice of One who spoke to him in chapter 1, calling him to come up to heavenly realms for a visit.

The Church Taken Up to Heaven

I believe that the call of John into heaven is a symbol of the WHOLE CHURCH being taken up into heaven. I take this position for four reasons:

1. The main theme of the first three chapters is Christ and his relationship to the church on earth. He communicated with the church through the apostle John. As such, John stands as the representative of all the Christians in those churches. John is now called into heaven, and I believe that, once again he, represents the whole church being called into heaven.

2. From chapter four on, we no longer have reference to the church on earth. The Bible tells us that one day soon, like John, we will hear the voice of the Son of God and be called up to heaven, "For the Lord himself will descend from heaven with a shout, with the voice of the archangel, and with the trumpet of God the dead in Christ shall rise first. Then we who are alive and remain shall be caught up together with them to meet the Lord in the air, and thus we shall always be with the Lord" (I Thess. 4:16-17).

3. Some commentators believe that the seven churches represent a chronology of church history for the past two thousand years, with Ephesus being the church of the post-apostolic period and Laodicea the church of the latter days just before the Lord's coming. If that is true, and I believe there's much cause for believing it, then the end of chapter three brings us right up to the time of the Lord's coming for his church.

4. When we consider the fact that, although the visions of Zechariah have much to say concerning the rest of the material in Revelation, they say NOTHING concerning the seven churches. This, too, gives weight to the view that here in chapter four the church has been caught up out of this world and is now resident in heaven.

The Throne Room Scene

Just as the way in which Christ appeared to John was of great significance in the opening scene of chapter one, so also does this scene lay the foundation for our understanding of what comes after. Let us consider the points:

1. "A throne was standing in heaven, and One sitting on the throne" (Rev.4:2)

What distinguishes the throne of God is an amazing display of light and colour. Emanating from the throne itself are the colours of jasper (crystal) and sardius (red). Around the throne a rainbow radiates its seven hues. Seven lamps of fire burn before the throne, adding the allure of leaping flames to the sight. These lamps are symbolic of the seven Spirits of God, which may refer to the sevenfold power of the Holy Spirit described in Is. 11:2. The crackling of lightning and the percussion of thunder lend the beauty of the storm to the awesome display, and the crystal sea in front of the throne reflects and magnifies it all many times over. Yet when it comes to describing the One on the throne, we do not get beyond this searing light. John tells us in his epistle that "God is light" (I John 1:5) and in his Gospel says "no man has seen God at any time" (John 1:18) and also adds "For God is spirit" (John 4:24).

2. **"And around the throne were twenty-four thrones and upon the thrones were twenty-four elders sitting, clothed in white garments and golden crowns on their heads:"**
(Rev.4:4)

While there is no mention of the church on earth between the fourth and nineteenth chapters of the book, there are twelve references to these elders who attend the heavenly throne room. I believe these elders represent the church in heaven for the following reasons:

a. They are given royal status. They sit on thrones and are given golden crowns on their heads (Rev.4:4). Angels are not promised such blessings in God's word, but the believers in Christ are (Rev. 1:6,3:21, 5:10; I Peter 2:9; Matt. 19:28).

b. They serve as priests. They wear white garments, the uniform of a priest (4:4). They have golden bowls full of incense which are the prayers of saints (5:8). Angels have never been given the responsibility in God's word to intercede in prayer, but the believers in Christ have (John 14:14; 15:17; 16:23). The church is also called a royal priesthood. (I Pet.2:9)

c. Twenty-four was the number of the elders of the priesthood in Israel. The twenty-four men listed in I Chron. 24 represented the whole priesthood. In a New Testament church, the leaders are called 'elders' (1 Tim. 5:17). It is fitting, then, that the church, which is the heavenly priesthood, should be represented by twenty-four elders.

3. "Four living creatures full of eyes in front and behind" (Rev.4:6)

These four creatures are similar to the ones who upheld the crystal expanse in Ezekiel's dream (Ez. 1:4-14), but there are some significant differences. The creatures in Ezekiel have four wings each; here they have six. The creatures in Ezekiel each have four faces. In Isaiah's vision of the throne room of God, there were six winged angels who hovered over the throne. It is possible, then, that the four-winged angels are cherubim (Gen. 3:24), whose task is to undergird the throne, and these mentioned here are seraphim, who overshadow the throne. At any rate, these angelic beings have four different faces. These four faces have been compared to the gospels in that they accurately picture the way in which Christ is presented in each gospel. As such, these four creatures not only give vocal worship to God (4:8,5:11-12), but their very appearance bears witness to the gospel, to the grace of God in providing a Saviour!

GOSPEL	VIEW OF CHRIST	FACE OF THE LIVING CREATURE
Matthew	King of Israel	The lion (king of beasts)
Mark	Servant of Jehovah	The calf (ox) (beast of burden)
Luke	Son of Man	The face of a man
John	Son of God	The eagle (bird of heaven)

The Saviour Appears in the Throne Room

Attention is now directed to a book in the hand of the One on the throne, "a book written inside and on the back, sealed up with seven seals" (Rev.5:1). A strong angel speaks out in the great hall of heaven, "Who is worthy to open the book and to break its seals?" For a time, there is silence, and it appears that no one is worthy to open the book, or to look into it. This brings a flood of tears to John, because he must realize the deep significance of this document for the people of God. Then one of the elders says to him, "Stop weeping; behold, the Lion of the tribe of Judah, the root of David, has overcome so as to open the book and its seven seals."
Two questions must be answered in order for us to understand what is happening here. The first is, "Who is the lamb?", and the second is, "What is the book?"

The Lamb

Those who know the New Testament at all will not see this identification as a problem. Indeed, they will wonder why the question was asked, seeing the answer is so plain from God's word. But that is the very reason for asking the question, that we might understand that while the immediate text does not positively identify who the lamb is, other scriptures positively answer the question. In fact, the apostle John himself tells us in John 1:29, "The next day he (John the Baptist) saw Jesus coming to him and said, "Behold, the Lamb of God who takes away the sins of the world!" The lamb is the Lord Jesus. The details of the description substantiate this.

1. "The Lion that is from the tribe of Judah"(Rev.5:5)

It was prophesied that the Messiah would come from the tribe of Judah (Gen. 49:9-10). The lion which was on the tribal standard of Judah symbolizes the power to rule as king.

2. "The Root of David"(Rev.5:5)

It was also prophesied that the Messiah would come from the family of David, the king (Is. 11:1-10).

3. "A Lamb standing, as if slain" (Rev.5:6)

Both of the above prophecies emphasize the great physical blessings that the Messiah would bring in for Israel as a kingdom of righteousness and peace is established. However, other Old Testament prophecies spoke of the Messiah who would suffer and die. In Isaiah 53, the Messiah is spoken of as a "lamb going to the slaughter", and by that act "bearing the sin of many". The slaying of the sacrificial lamb on the Altar of Sacrifice was the central act of worship in the tabernacle (and later in the temple). In fact, there was to be a sacrificed lamb burning on the altar at all times (Ex. 29:38-42). This reaffirmed the principle of God's dealing with sin, "For the life of the flesh is in the blood and I have given it to you on the altar to make atonement for your souls; for it is the blood by reason of the life that makes atonement" (Lev. 17:11). However, animal sacrifices could never fully take away sins, as evidenced by the fact that they had to be repeated year after year (Heb. 10:1-4).

These sacrifices were only a symbol of the one perfect sacrifice for sins that would be accomplished by the Messiah. That is why John the Baptist called Jesus "the Lamb of God". By his death on the cross He would take away the sins of the world and make it possible for all who trust in Him to be saved (Heb. 10:14).

But this Lamb is no longer dead! He is very much alive! He has risen in triumph from the dead and is alive forevermore (Rev. 1:15). However, he appears "as if slain". In other words, He bears the marks of His suffering, just as He bore them when He appeared to the disciples after the resurrection (John 20:26-28). These precious marks will forever identify Him as Saviour.

4. "Having seven horns and seven eyes"(Rev. 5:9)

Horns speak of strength and eyes speak of wisdom. The number seven would suggest the idea of perfection of strength (omnipotence) and perfection of wisdom (omniscience). But we are given a sure interpretation in the text itself, for it says the horns and eyes represent the seven Spirits of God sent out into all the earth. This is a reference to the intimate relationship between the Saviour and the Holy Spirit which so characterized the earthly life of Christ (Luke 4:1).

The Book

We have already heard of a book(scroll) in the Revelation. It is the one containing the seven letters to the seven churches (Rev. 1:11). This book is different in that it is not a message which John is asked to write; it is written already. Also, it is sealed up with seven seals. What else are we able to learn about this book that will help us to determine what it is?

1. It is a book of prophecy, a book of future events of history (Rev.6:1-8:8).

2. It is originally in the hands of the Father (Rev. 5:1). He does not open the book, but controls the timing of its opening (Acts 1:6-7).

3. It is the Lamb who takes the book and breaks its seal (Rev.5:7, 6:1). We are told that only He is worthy to do this because he was slain and has purchased for God with his blood, men from every tribe and tongue and people and nation (Rev. 5:9). It is the "saviourhood" of the Lord that qualifies him to open the book. His precious blood was the only thing that could pay the price for man's sin, and he willingly paid it (I Pet. 1:18-19).

Books! Books! Books!

There are several accounts in Scripture concerning books which shed light on what is happening here.

1. A book of judgment

We read in Luke 4:16 – 30 an account of Jesus' early ministry. After his baptism and temptation, Jesus returned to his hometown of Nazareth, and on the Sabbath he entered the synagogue and stood to read. The book of the prophet Isaiah was handed to him, and he read Is. 61:1-2. However, he stopped in the middle of the reading and CLOSED THE BOOK. Where did he stop? He had just finished reading how the Messiah would come to preach the gospel in grace and mercy, and to proclaim the acceptable year of the Lord. Then he said, "Today this scripture has been fulfilled in your hearing". He did not read the following phrase, "and the day of vengeance of our God". Why? Because that would not be fulfilled until He came back a second time.

The breaking of the seals, the opening of the closed book will initiate "the day of vengeance of our God", a time of great sorrow and destruction. However, it will also usher in final salvation to Israel because the following verses in Isaiah 61 describe the comfort and blessing God will extend to Zion.

2. A sealed book

There is an intriguing reference to a sealed book in Isaiah 29:11. "The entire vision shall be to you like the words of a SEALED book, which when they give it to the one who is literate, saying, "Please read this", he will say, "I cannot, for it is sealed." The vision is evidently the prophecy of Isaiah (Is. 1:1). The sealing of the prophecy is symbolic of the inability of the Jews to understand its contents. They are unable because God has blinded their eyes to understand. "The Lord has poured over you a spirit of deep sleep; he has shut your eyes, the prophets; he has covered your heads, the seers" (Is. 29:10).

That has been the spiritual situation of the Jews since they rejected the law of God and the testimony of the prophets, in order to go after the gods of other nations (Is. 8:16-21). That is the curse that was pronounced by the Lord through Isaiah (Is. 6:9-13). It was the curse on their minds and hearts that existed in Christ's day (Matt.13:13-15) and still exists.

However, the text in Isaiah 29 goes on to say, "And on that day the deaf shall hear the words of the book, and out of their gloom and darkness the eyes of the blind shall see" (Is. 29:18). The New Testament corroborates this in Romans 11:25-26. "A partial hardening has happened to Israel until the fullness of the Gentiles has come in; and thus all Israel will be saved."

When the Lord breaks the seals of the book in Revelation

chapter 5, He is not revealing something that is a mystery
to us, because we are able to read today exactly what
is contained in these seals. When He breaks the seals,
the Saviour is symbolically revealing to the Jews what
they were blinded from seeing in the prophecy of Isaiah.
I believe we have a physical illustration of this truth in
the Lord's dealing with Saul in Acts 9. Saul is judicially
blinded by the Lord. For three days he is without sight
until Ananias, the servant of the Lord, comes to him
with a message of healing and the promise of the filling
of the Holy Spirit. "Immediately, there fell from his eyes
something like scales, and he regained his sight, and arose
and was baptized" (Acts9:18).

Other Old Testament prophets present this same scenario.

Daniel was told that the words of his book are to be
CONCEALED AND SEALED UP until the end of time
(Dan.12:4). At that time the curse will be lifted, and "many
will run to and fro and knowledge shall be increased". This
sealing is mentioned again in verse 9 as being "until the
end of time." Israel would then be "purged, purified, and
refined", words which connote trial and judgment. That
testing would create two groups of people, the wicked
ones without understanding, and those with insight
who understand. The ones who understand will turn in

repentance and faith to the Saviour and be rescued out of their trials (Is. 35:5).

3. A book of salvation

A third reference to a sealed book or scroll is in Jeremiah 32. As the armies of Babylon were closing in on Jerusalem, Jeremiah was told to buy a portion of land near Jerusalem that belonged to his nephew, Hanamel, but now rested in enemy hands. Hanamel was understandably anxious to unload what seemed to him a worthless piece of real estate. However, since Jeremiah had the first right to buy it (he being a close relative), and since God had told him to do so, he weighed out seventeen shekels of silver for it and signed the deed. Jeremiah then told Baruch to hide the SEALED DEED in an earthenware jar "that it may last a long time."

The meaning of all this is explained by the Lord, "For just as I brought all this great disaster on this people, so I am going to bring on them all the good that I am promising them. And fields shall be bought in this land of which you say, "It is a desolation..." (Jer.32:42-43). Just as Jeremiah had the right to buy the land because he was a near relative, so the Lord Jesus became a man that he might be related to us (Heb. 2:17). And just as Jeremiah paid the full price of purchase, so Jesus paid the price of his precious blood at the cross that he might buy back those who, like Hanamel's land, had fallen into enemy hands (I Pet. 1:18-19). In the future, Israel, in their extremity, will repent and return to the Saviour and experience the full physical and spiritual blessings spoken by the prophets.

In conclusion, the book is the sum of the Old Testament prophecy, revealing future events. That is the book that Jesus will read from again. It is there, in Isaiah and Ezekiel and Jeremiah, that the Jews of a coming day will learn of God's plan of judgment and eventual blessing, as their eyes are opened to understanding the truth.

THE SEVEN SEAL JUDGMENTS

The First Four Seals

Four horses with their riders are called onto the scene of world history by the four living creatures. This rider on a white steed is a regal warrior. He comes in conquest. Some identify this one with the Messiah king (Rev. 19:11). However, although the designation is not clear at this point, we have only to see what follows this rider to realize that he does not bring the blessing of heaven, but rather the curse of hell. It is far more likely that this represents the antichrist, a false messiah, who will come to deceive the world.

The 'Gospel' of the Antichrist

The Four Gospels of Christ		The Four "Gospels" of the Antichrist
First living creature Like a lion = Christ as King of Kings as seen in Matthew	calls up	Man on white horse who is crowned = Antichrist the evil king
Second living creature Like a calf or ox = Christ serving men as seen in Mark	calls up	Man on red horse Antichrist brings war = Men slaying one another
Third living creature Like a man = Christ fellowshipping with others at the table as seen in Luke	calls up	Man on black horse brings famine but spares luxury goods= society polarized
Fourth living creature Like an eagle = Christ as God who brings men Life and Heaven as seen in John	calls up	Men on Ashen horse, who are Death and Hades, the final end of the 'gospel' of the antichrist

The four horses are called up by the four living creatures. As we have already seen, there is a striking correspondence between these four living creatures and the display of Christ as Saviour as recorded in the gospels. When Jesus came to his own they rejected Him. So now they will be given a false saviour, one whose gospel is the exact opposite of the true gospel. In the chart you will notice the contrast between the program of the true Saviour and the false.

The Fifth Seal- Martyrdom

The majority of Jews will accept the Antichrist as a great deliverer and make a covenant of peace with him (Dan. 9:27). They will be totally deceived by his 'gospel' of peace and security. But this deceiver will betray them, and what seemed like a peace treaty, will become a covenant with death and Sheol (Is. 28:15).

A minority of Jews whose hearts and minds have been opened by the breaking of the seals will hold true to the holy covenant, their commitment to the true God, and because of this they will suffer great persecution (Dan.11:31-35). In Revelation 6:9, they are seen underneath the altar in the temple in heaven. These faithful disciples of the Lamb have made the final sacrifice, and now they are identified with that sacred place where the blood of another innocent victim (Jesus) was shed.

Not in vain has their blood been shed, for it is precious in the sight of God (Ps. 72:14, 116:15). They cry for judgment on their enemies and ask, "How long?" But the patience of God waits yet, and others must join them under that altar before the account is settled. Notice that there is a specific number of those to be martyred; it is under the Lord's control.

The Sixth Seal- Cosmic Storm

The awesome storm described here takes us right up to the second coming of the Lord. The extinguishing of the light of the sun (Rev.6:12), is the prelude to the appearance of the Saviour (Is. 13:9-10; Joel 2:30-31; Matt.24:29). The imagery of the scroll is again brought out, for it says, "the sky was split apart like a scroll when it is rolled up" (Is. 34:4). The enemies of the Lamb now cower in the caves and among the rocks (Is. 2:10-21). The great day of his wrath has come, and "who is able to stand?" (Is. 63:4).

Notice, by the way, how many cross references are from Isaiah in this section of Revelation. This is because Isaiah is pre-eminently the prophet of salvation. For instance, the word 'salvation' is mentioned twenty-eight times in Isaiah and only seven times in all the rest of the Old Testament prophets.

The Sealed on Earth and the Blessed in Heaven

Having brought us right up to the time of the Lord's return, John's attention is now turned to the two groups of people in Revelation 7. The first group are the Jews because the Spirit goes to great lengths to emphasize that the 144,000 are from the tribes of Israel, even to naming the tribes and spelling out that 12,000 come from each tribe. It is therefore amazing that a certain religious body today should claim that the 144,000 are Gentiles of their own sect! Why are these 144,000 protected? I believe it is because of their work of evangelism. They will "preach the gospel of the kingdom in the whole world as a testimony to all the nations, and then the end will come" (Matthew 24:14).

This group of Jews is singled out for divine protection. Before the four angels of God release the four winds of earth, symbolizing the great storm of trouble to come, these precious ones are marked with the seal of the living God on their foreheads. Such a sealing appears in Ezekiel, where those who were to be physically spared from the onslaught of the angelic contingent were similarly marked (Ez. 9:1-11). Note once again that the imagery of SEALS comes into play. The seals on the scroll are broken by the power of the Lamb, but these seals guarantee complete protection by that same power.

The second group of people are the great harvest

resulting from their evangelism. They are Gentiles from all the nations, "a great multitude, which no one could count"(Rev.7:9). They are identified as those who have gone through a great tribulation. Evidently, these are ones who have heard the gospel of salvation in Christ and have trusted in Him, for it says, "They have washed their robes and made them white in the blood of the Lamb"(Rev.7:14). We will return to this wonderful scene in a later chapter.

The Zechariah Connection

The first four visions of Zechariah (Zech.18-2:13) are united by a single theme, the Lord will never abandon Jerusalem but will save it in the end. These visions proclaim the Lord as Saviour of his people. This same theme dominates the second section of Revelation from chapter four through seven.

The similarities are many.

1. Just as the seals open with the four horsemen, so also does Zechariah have four horsemen (Zech. 1:7-17). The four horsemen of Zechariah are angelic beings under the leadership of the Angel of the Lord, who is none other than the Lord Jesus (Ex. 20:20-23). Their concern is for Israel which is in bondage to the Gentile nations.

2. The angel of the Lord cries, "How long?" (Zech. 1:12), just as the martyrs of the fifth seal cry.

3. The second vision of Zechariah (Zech. 1:18-21) refers to four horns (polical power) which have scattered Judah, Israel, and Jerusalem. These may represent the four great world empires of Daniel's prophecy: Babylon, Persia, Greece, and Rome. In Revelation, the final world power ruled by the rider on the white horse is allowed to afflict the Jews.

4. In the third vision, four craftsmen in turn are used by God to overthrow these nations. For instance, Cyrus of Medo-Persia was the 'craftsman' in the hands of God to overthrow the Babylonian empire (Is.45:1). Similarly, in the sixth seal, God deals with the nations of the end times who have vaunted themselves against the nation of Israel (Rev. 6:12-17).

5. In the fourth vision of Zechariah (Zech. 2:1-13), the Lord measures Israel for blessing and promises to be a 'wall of fire' about her. Similarly, in Revelation, the Jews are given a sign of the Lord's physical keeping, a seal on their foreheads.

6. In Zechariah 2:6, the Jews are scattered 'as the four winds of the heavens'. In Revelation 7:1-2, the four winds of the earth now turn to wreak havoc on all except the chosen of God.

7. In Zechariah 2:11, "many nations will join themselves to the Lord in that day and will become my people." This is exactly what happens in Revelation 7:9-17, where people from all nations are blessed in the Lamb's presence.

8. In Zechariah's first four visions, the number four is prominent: the four horsemen, four horns, four craftsmen, four winds of heaven. In Revelation 4 to 7, the number four is also prominent: four living creatures, four horsemen, and authority is given over a fourth of the earth.

The Tabernacle Connection: The Altar of Sacrifice

Throughout this section, Christ is viewed as the Saviour. Ten times he is called the Lamb (twenty-eight times in all of Revelation) and reference is made to his death four times (Rev. 5:6, 9, 12, 7:14). Armed only with this information, we should be able to identify which article of tabernacle furniture is being featured here. The place where the lambs were offered was the Altar of Sacrifice. However, there is direct reference to it in Revelation 7:9 where, as we have seen, the martyrs are pictured as being under the altar.

One of the distinctives of the altar was its four horns, one on each corner (Ex. 29:12). It is noteworthy that in Zechariah's third vision there were four horns to represent the enemies of the Jews. In contrast, the horns of the altar represent refuge and mercy (1 Kings 1:50-51), so it is understandable that the martyrs would resort to such a spot.

Invitation to Worship

So many Christian hymns of worship have come out of this section of Revelation that many of the verses are familiar. Knowing now the significance of the number seven, it should not surprise us that there are seven great expressions of praise to God and to the Lamb. (Rev. 4:8, 11, 5:9-10, 12, 13, 7:10,12). The twenty-four elders, the four living creatures, myriads of angels, and the redeemed from the nations join with all created things to worship Him who alone is worthy.

Worship begins with appreciation of WHO GOD IS. In chapter four they give praise to the majestic Creator of heaven and earth. Worship expands greatly in chapter five when we learn WHAT GOD HAS DONE though the work of the Lamb. John was weeping because no one was able to break the seal and open the book, in order to bring salvation to Israel. But just as Christ's precious blood has purchased salvation for the church, so that cleansing tide will reach even to the "survivors of Israel" (Is. 4:2-4). They will be saved in the same way all others have ever been saved from eternal judgment, by claiming the value of the precious blood of Christ to cleanse them from sin. Worship reaches its fullest expression in chapter seven with the appreciation of WHO THE LAMB IS. Over 30 times Isaiah uses the expression "no one", "none", or "no other" to emphasize that there is only one Saviour, and He is God (i.e., Is. 43:11). When we see the Lamb "in the center of the throne" we are brought to the full understanding of who this One is who was slain for us, IMMANUEL, God with us!

Vision III

CHRIST

THE GREAT HIGH PRIEST

The 7 Trumpet Judgments

Vision III
The Great High Priest

The eighth chapter begins the third section of Revelation. Verse three introduces one called an angel, who is doing the work of a priest, standing at the Altar of Incense. There is much disagreement among commentators as to who this angel is. Some say it is only an angel, others believe it is Jesus Himself. I hold to the second view. However, since there is this difference of opinion, we will discuss three arguments which support our view.

1.   The Argument of Precedence

Those arguing that the angel can't be Jesus say so because He doesn't appear as an angel anywhere else in the New Testament. However, the answer to this is that the book of Revelation is not just a New Testament book. Rather, it is a summary book of both Old and New Testaments as we have already seen. Old Testament symbols abound, perhaps because the ones who will in future use this book as a survival guide, that is, the Jews of the tribulation period, will be thoroughly versed in the Old Testament.

In the Old Testament, there was a mysterious person who appeared a number of times to various people, called the ANGEL OF THE LORD. In Judges 2:1-5 the Angel of the Lord says to Israel, "I brought you up out of Egypt ...".

Notice He did not say, "Thus says the Lord" to preface His remarks, as the prophets did who spoke in the name of the Lord. This angel says in effect, "It was I who brought you up out of Egypt." Notice also that He made a covenant with Israel which he calls "MY COVENANT." I don't find any angels making covenants with men in all of scripture. We are to understand then, that the Angel of the Lord is the Lord Himself. In Isaiah 63:9, He is also called "the Angel of His Presence" and named as the Saviour of Israel.

In Gen.16, the Angel of the Lord appears to Hagar, and verse 13 says, "She called the name of the Lord who spoke to her, "You are a God who sees"". In Chapter 18, He appears to Abraham in company with two angels. (see Gen. 19:1). As Abraham viewed them from afar, they appeared as three men, one indistinguishable from the other, but when he approached them, he understood that One was indeed the Lord. This is what we have in Revelation 8. On first impression, this One appears to be only another angel. But, on closer inspection, the real truth becomes known to us.

In Judges 13, the Angel of the Lord appears to Manoah, the father of Samson, and, in course of conversation, reveals His name as "Wonderful"(vs. 18). Only one person bears this divine Name. It is the Messiah of Israel, Jesus Christ Himself (Isaiah 9:6). Therefore, by the argument of

PRECEDENCE we conclude that it is reasonable to see the angel in Revelation 8 as Jesus.

2.   The Argument of Prophecy

The last book of the Old Testament, as we know it, is Malachi, a prophet whose name is taken from the Hebrew word "Malak", meaning "messenger". This is also the same word for "angel" in Hebrew. The term "angel", then, has a general meaning of "messenger", as well as a specific reference to a particular group of created beings. Malachi's name has personal meaning for himself in that he was a messenger sent from God with a message to the people. His message included the prophecy that two more messengers (Malaki) would come from God. In Malachi 3:1, God says, "Behold, I am going to send my messenger, and he will clear the way before Me". This is undoubtedly John the Baptist whose ministry prepared the way for the Messiah. However, God then speaks of the second messenger in the same verse, "And the Lord whom you seek will suddenly come to His temple; and the messenger (angel) of the covenant, in whom you delight, behold He is coming.." This certainly refers to Jesus and may have been understood to have been completely fulfilled at His first coming. However, the verses which follow seem to indicate something else. "But who can endure the day of His coming? And who can stand when He appears? For He is like a refiner's fire and like a fuller's soap. And He will sit as a smelter and purifier of silver, and He will purify the sons of Levi, and refine them like gold and silver, so that they may present to the Lord offerings in righteousness" (Mal 3:2-3). This was not accomplished at His first coming and remains to be fulfilled when He comes again. The Messenger of the Covenant is thus another designation of Jesus, the Angel of the Lord. He is to come as such in the future, to purify and refine His people.

We conclude that this angel is none other than Jesus, our Great High priest. This is the argument of prophecy.

3.   The Argument of Function

Before we leave the reference in Malachi, it is important to note the function of the Messenger of the Covenant. He comes to His temple. And when He comes, His work will be to purify the sons of Levi in order that they may present to the Lord offerings in righteousness. The angel's work is therefore tied in with the priestly service of the temple. In Mal. 2:7, the priest is specifically called "the messenger of the Lord of Hosts". Now, this is exactly what is happening in Revelation 8!

The Tabernacle Connection: The Altar of Incense

We must review the priestly ministry in regard to the Altar of Incense in order to understand what is going on in our text. Aaron was instructed to burn incense morning and evening on the Altar of Incense located in the Holy Place in front of the veil (Ex.30:1-8). In Ps. 141:2, King David likens his prayer going up to God to incense rising. Furthermore, in Luke 1:9-10 we hear how Zecharias, a priest of Israel, entered the Holy Place of the temple to burn incense, while "the whole multitude of the people were in prayer outside at the hour of the incense offering." Once again, the golden altar and the incense rising from it are associated with prayer. While the multitude prayed outside, one priest entered the Holy Place on their behalf to intercede for them before God. Imagine the holy hush and the bowed heads as the people waited in prayerful expectation. The re-emergence of the priest was the sign that their priest had been accepted in God's presence, and their prayers had been heard. That is why there was such amazement and wonder amongst the people when Zecharias failed to appear in time (Luke 1:21). That is also most likely why, in Rev. 8:1, there is silence in heaven for about half an hour. It is the hour of prayer, and the priest is in the Holy Place in the heavenly temple, praying on behalf of the people.

Now, the question to ask at this point is, "Did God ever commit to angels the ministry of prayer and intercession?" We know that "angels are ministering spirits sent out to render service for the sake of those who will inherit salvation" (Heb.11:4). However, were they ever asked to pray for men? In Rev. 15:6, they are clothed in priestly garb and sent out of the temple on an errand of judgment. But, as to a ministry of prayer and intercession, the Scriptures are silent. However, where Scripture is not silent is in emphasizing and re-emphasizing the great truth that there is "one God, and one mediator between God and men, the man Christ Jesus" (I Tim. 2-5). The book of Hebrews presents the qualifications for the heavenly priesthood. The first qualification is that "He had to be made like His brethren in all things, that He might become a merciful and faithful high priest in things pertaining to God" (Heb. 2:17).

When the function of this One at the Altar of Incense is considered, it is clear that we are once again seeing our Great High Priest, Jesus Christ. In heaven, He still carries on the same ministry of intercession that He began while here on earth (John 17:9, 20, Luke 22:32). He, and He alone, is the One who intercedes for us before God (Heb 7:25, Rom. 8:27, 34).

We conclude that this angel is none other than Jesus, our Great High Priest. This is the argument of function.

The High Priest and His Priesthood

Someone might ask, "For whom is Christ interceding?" Though the church is now in heaven, there are still those on the earth who belong to the Lord. These are both converted Jews and Gentiles, as we saw in chapter 7. As He now prays for us, so He will pray for them. And it is clear to see that the redeemed saints in heaven engage in this ministry with their Lord. Several times they are called priests (Rev 1:6, 5:10). In chapter 5, verse 8, the 24 elders, who represent the priesthood of the church in heaven, are actually carrying golden bowls full of incense representing their prayers. What a tremendous privilege is ours to be engaged in the ministry of intercession under the authority of Jesus, our High Priest! At the close of the book of Job, after Job learns how great his God is, the Lord invites him to pray (Job 42:7:9). He is not to pray for himself now, but for his three friends who are under God's wrath for their unjust criticism of Job. It is Job's prayer that is the key to their acceptance before God. His intercession is the key that unleashes the power of God to restore and bless.

The Lord indicates many times over that our power today also lies in prayer. Jesus said, "Truly, truly, I say to you, if you shall ask the Father for anything, He will give it to you in My Name" (John 16:23). The apostle Paul knew this power both in the giving of prayer for others (Phil. 1:9), and the receiving of it for his own needs (Phil. 1:19). Why do we then scorn our high privilege and calling? Why do we not pray? If we could only get into our minds that this is what our Lord is doing right now, this is what He holds of first importance right now, then we who say we follow Christ would make this work of intercession our priority as well.

The Zechariah Connection

Zechariah 3 is the vision of Joshua the High Priest. However, Joshua is not the only high priest in this passage. There is One called the Angel of the Lord who is interceding for him, just as a lawyer would in a court of law. And who might this be? Surely it is Jesus. "And if anyone sins, we have an advocate with the Father, Jesus Christ the Righteous ..." (I John 2:1). There is also another lawyer in this scene, Satan himself, who is "the accuser of our brethren ... who accuses them before our God, day and night" (Rev. 12:10). He is the attorney for the opposition, the high priest of darkness. Joshua's filthy garments symbolize that he was a sinner, as were all the high priests of Israel prior to the coming of the Holy One. That is why it was necessary, in the ceremony of the tabernacle, for the priest to first bring a sin offering for himself before he could bring a sin offering on behalf of the people (Lev. 9:8).

The Angel of the Lord does three things for Joshua here. First, He rescues him from the fire. Second, He clothes him as a priest. Third, He reaffirms his authority, along with the other priests, to serve in the house of the Lord. This is a prophecy in picture form of what Jesus will do for the nation of Israel in a coming day. (Notice the reference to "Jerusalem" in verse 2 and "the land" in verse 9). He who God calls "my servant the Branch" (3:8) will rescue them, cleanse them and make them His priests once again. This is the very process that is going on in the book of Revelation! The Jewish remnant is being purged in order that they might be the priests of God on this earth (Malachi 3:1-5).

The Fire of the Altar

Fire is one of the great destructive forces known to man. It is a symbol of judgment all through the Scripture. John the Baptist prophesied that the Messiah would baptize with the Holy Spirit and with fire, and that He would burn up the chaff with unquenchable fire (Matt. 3:11-12). Here, then, is the beginning of that fiery judgment. Having just offered incense at the altar, an act of love and mercy for His own, the High Priest now turns His attention to an unbelieving world, and burning coals of judgment are cast from the golden censer down onto the earth.

The Rebellion of Korah

For an appreciation of this event, we refer back yet again to the Old Testament, to Numbers 16. This chapter records the rebellion of the sons of Korah. Korah was a Levite and he and his family shared an honourable role in the service of the tabernacle. However, they were not sons of Aaron, and therefore not qualified to be priests, but they coveted the priesthood and openly rebelled against Moses and Aaron. So Moses asked them to appear with censers, not the golden censers of the priest, but the brass censers of the Levite. When they did, God brought judgment both from above and below. First, the ground opened up to swallow the ringleaders. Next, fire came from above to consume the rest of the rebels. Then Aaron was instructed to scatter the coals from their censers on the earth, a fitting symbol of the judgment that preceded. When the children of Israel grumbled at this harsh judgment, immediately a deadly plague broke out in the whole camp. So, Moses said to Aaron, "Take your censer and put in it fire from the altar, and lay incense on it; then bring it quickly to the congregation and make atonement for them, for wrath has gone forth from the Lord, the plague has begun" (Numbers 16:46). Then it says that "Aaron took His stand between the dead and the living, so that the plague was checked."

Although the order of events is changed in Revelation 8, the similarities are many.

1. The problem was rebellion against God's priest. This is the very reason for the trumpet judgments. In Rev. 9:20, it shows the world caught up in prayer to idols and the worship of demons.

2. The test of authority was that both sides were to appear with censers of burning incense. In Rev. 9:2, a demonic being, symbolized by a star, is given authority to open the bottomless pit, and smoke goes up out of the pit like the smoke of a great furnace. This smoke contrasts with the smoke of the altar in Rev 8:4; it is the devil's incense! In Rev. 9:15-19, a great army of devil-inspired horsemen cause a third of mankind to be killed by the fire and smoke and brimstone that proceed from their mouths. This is the fire of the devil's censer!

3. God judged the imposters from above and below. Similarly, in Rev. 8, fire and judgment falls from above in various forms, and then rises from beneath:

a.   Hail and fire mixed with blood (1st trumpet).
b.   A great mountain burning with fire (2nd trumpet).
c.   A great star falls from heaven burning like a torch (3rd trumpet).
d.   The sun, moon and stars smitten and the earth darkened (4th trumpet).
e.   A great storm from the temple of God (7th trumpet).
f.   Judgment also rises from beneath; a devilish horde ascending from the bottomless pit (5th trumpet).

4. The coals from the censers are scattered abroad as a symbol of the fiery devastation of divine judgment.
 So too, in Rev. 8:5, the High Priest initiates the trumpet judgments by scattering the burning coals from the censer onto the earth.

5. The high priest takes His stand between the dead and the living to intercede on their behalf. In Rev. 8, the High Priest does exactly the same thing in order to save His own out of the plague on the earth. His judgments upon the world of the ungodly are tempered by a tender care for His own in the midst of the trial (9:4). They are divinely protected from the fire!

Coals in Ezekiel

A second Old Testament reference gives us a similar

understanding of the significance of scattering coals. In Ezekiel 9, after God had given Ezekiel a glimpse of the way the people of Israel were desecrating His temple, six angels and a man clothed in linen appear to the prophet. This man is not identified save for the fact that the linen he wears is suggestive of a priest. He is told by God to go through the city of Jerusalem and put a mark on all who sorrow over the sin of Israel. The angels follow behind to destroy all who are left unmarked. In chapter 10, this man clothed in linen enters the very throne room of God and is given coals of fire which originate from between the cherubim. He exits with these coals and scatters them over the city as a symbol of divine judgment.

Although internal evidence is lacking, it is nonetheless possible that this man clothed in linen is another picture of the Lord Jesus in His priestly ministry.

Priests, Trumpets and Judgment

We have seen how the stories of Korah and Ezekiel shed light on this passage in Revelation. Another great Old Testament story is pictured here as well, one that highlights priests, trumpets and judgment. It's the story of the Battle of Jericho, in case you hadn't guessed.

Jericho was the first great test of Joshua's army in the conquest of the promised land. But before Joshua could draw up his own battle plan, he was visited by a man identifying himself as Captain of the Host of the Lord

(Josh. 5:13–15). That this man was the Lord is evidenced by the fact that Joshua was told to remove his sandals because he was standing on holy ground, just as Moses had been instructed when talking with God before the burning bush.

From the Lord, Joshua received what may have impressed him as a very strange and unworkable battle plan. He was told to march his men around the city once each day for six days, then, on the seventh day, they were to march around seven times. The only noise was to be made by seven priests blowing seven trumpets as they led the army. At the conclusion of the seventh circuit on the seventh day, the priests were to make a long blast with their rams' horns and this was the signal for the army of Israel to shout. When they followed these orders, the walls of Jericho came tumbling down and the city was taken.

The comparisons with the action of Rev. 8 are very instructive.

1. The days of battle were seven and the seventh day contained seven circuits of the city. In Revelation 8, we have just finished the judgments of the seven seals and out of them come seven trumpets. The battle plan of the Lord in Revelation is the same as that for Jericho!

2. The seven priests were the ones who had the trumpets and blew them on instruction. In Revelation 8, the Lord

Jesus, our High Priest, initiates the action. Notice in Rev. 9: 13-14, it is the voice from the four horns of the golden altar (where Jesus is standing) which directs the sixth trumpeter. Immediately, seven angels clothed as priests and bearing seven trumpets begin to sound. Why were they clothed as priests? Because the real enemy was a spiritual force of evil, not the physical might of the Canaanites of Jericho. The real wall was not the physical walls of the city of Jericho but the spiritual stronghold of the forces of darkness to whom these people gave homage. When one is fighting such an enemy, he does not need physical weapons but rather spiritual ones. Paul says in II Cor. 10:3-4, "For though we walk in the flesh, we do not war according to the flesh, for the weapons of our warfare are not of the flesh, but divinely powerful for the destruction of forces."

3. The army of Israel was to walk in silence for all the circuits except the last. When the final trumpet blew, then they were to shout in triumph. In Revelation 8. the Lord's people are in silence as their High Priest intercedes for His own (8:1), silence but not inactivity, because they are in prayer. (I suspect the armies of Joshua were similarly in prayer as they quietly circled the city). However, at the final trumpet, they break into loud voices and worship God for His victory (Rev. 11:15-17). In our spiritual warfare today, we would do well to remember this lesson, "in quietness and trust is your strength" (Is. 30:15). It is not the quietness of slumber or fear, but rather the quietness of a praying and trusting heart. Note also the silence enjoined upon all flesh in Zech. 2:13, just before the Lord appears in His high priestly role.

The Signal Trumpets of the Priests

In II Chr. 13, there is recorded a battle between King Abijah of Judah and King Jeroboam of Israel. Abijah was outnumbered two to one, but still went out boldly to do battle because he believed the Lord was on his side. "Now behold, God is with us at our head, and His priests with the signal trumpets to sound the alarm against you." These trumpets were, as we have already seen in the account of the battle of Jericho, the signal for warfare. They not only signalled the beginning of conflict but, because they were blown by priests, also served to remind the people of the spiritual conflict behind the physical one. In the case of Abijah and Jeroboam, Jeroboam had introduced the idolatrous worship of the golden calves into Israel, and had set up a new priesthood to serve the people in their apostasy. And so, when the signal trumpets were blown just as at Jericho, God supernaturally intervened and routed Jeroboam and all Israel before Abijah and Judah.

Seven Trumpet Judgments

In the seal judgments, God is allowing man to have his day, and the evil and destruction there are, generally speaking, the result of man's malevolence. The action of the seal judgments is easy enough to follow because it is the stuff of the daily newspaper and TV newscasts ... world leaders with promises of peace, and their great armies that give the lie to their words, famine in war torn areas, pestilence and death, the slaughter of innocents, etc. However, with the trumpet judgments the SUPERNATURAL ELEMENT becomes more pronounced. The Lord is indeed directing the judgment, however, He is no longer using human agencies, but rather diabolic ones. In the trumpet judgments, Christ is giving a measure of freedom to the devil to create havoc on the earth. That is why it is more difficult to interpret what is going on with certainty, because natural and supernatural are mixed together.

The second trumpet reveals something like a mountain burning with fire being thrown into the sea, with the result that a third of the sea becomes blood, a third of the sea life dies, and a third of the ships are destroyed. Once again, a literal rendering is possible. However, at the third trumpet, a star called Wormwood, falls from heaven and pollutes rivers and springs causing many men to die. This is followed in the fifth trumpet by the statement, "I saw a star from heaven which had fallen to the earth", and the star is an angelic person. Is the star of the third trumpet and that of the fifth trumpet one and the same?

In the fourth trumpet, a third of the luminaries in the heavens are darkened for a third of both day and night. In Rev. 12:3-4, a sign in heaven shows a great red dragon whose tail sweeps away a third of the stars of heaven and throws them to the earth. Are these to be equated with the third of the stars in the 4th trumpet? In Rev. 12, it appears that the stars are angelic beings, but are they so in Rev. 9? Perhaps the events of the trumpet judgments are entirely literal and physical and are but the reflection of the events taking place in the spirit world. We can only guess.

It appears that the fifth judgment is a plague of evil spirits upon the earth, and not just locusts and scorpions. They originate from the bottomless pit and have as king over them an angel called Apollyon which means "destruction". Their target is restricted to only those men who do not have the seal of God on their foreheads. The sixth judgment may be a literal army of men, perhaps the armies of the great Eastern nations like China, India, and Japan, which lie beyond the Euphrates River. Also, the number of the horsemen (two hundred million), is not beyond the means of these very populated countries. However, the description of the armies is highly symbolic and suggests that we are dealing once again with demonic hordes.The repetition of the fraction 1/3 seems to indicate an increase in intensity of judgment over the seal judgments since the fraction there is 1/4. (6:8)

No doubt all of these difficulties in interpretation will be cleared up as the events overtake the people of that day. Whatever these trumpets do mean, this we know for certain, that they will surely come to pass, and they will be horrific. The most amazing and sobering aspect of all this, though, is not what is going to happen, but rather, mankind's reaction to what happens. Having experienced all of the judgment of God thus far described, the heart of man is still unrepentant, and set in its perversity and evil (9:20-21).

VISION IV

CHRIST

THE GREAT PROPHET

Prophesy Again
The Prophet John
Seven Persons from Prophecy
Moses
Elijah
Michael
Israel
Satan
Beast from Sea
Beast From Land

Vision IV

Christ The Great Prophet

With chapter ten, we come to the central picture of Christ in the book, the fourth of seven. It is the picture of Christ as the great prophet of God. What a fitting centerpiece for a book of prophecy! Here John is saying in effect, "These are not my words, but the words of Him who sent me." Here God is saying, "This is my beloved Son, in whom I am well pleased, listen to him."

Another Strong Angel

The first question to answer is, "Who is this angel'? Having advanced the three arguments in the preceding chapter that Jesus appears as an angel, I will not repeat them here. Suffice to say, I believe that this angel also is Jesus. Some might argue that if this is Jesus, why does John refer to him as "another angel", and not the same one as in chapter eight? The answer, I believe, is that Jesus is now dressed for a different part. When we examine all the evidence for this angel being Jesus, how He looks, what He says, and what He does, we should reply as the two disciples did on the road to Emmaus, who had at first mistaken the identity of the Lord, "Were not our hearts burning within us while He was speaking to us on the road, while He was explaining the scriptures to us?" (Luke24:32)

89

<h1 style="text-align:center">What He Looks Like</h1>

1. Clothed with a cloud (Rev. 10:1)

This is not the first time Jesus is associated with clouds in Revelation (1:7), nor will it be the last (Rev.14:14). The cloud is a symbol of divine presence. God provided a cloud for the children of Israel to go before them and guide them through the desert (Ex. 13:21-22). When Moses finished building the tabernacle "the cloud covered the tent of meeting, and the glory of the Lord filled the tabernacle" (Ex. 40:34). God appeared to Moses and spoke to him in this cloud (Ex. 9:10). When God spoke to affirm the unique prophetic ministry of His Son on the Mount of Transfiguration, a cloud formed and overshadowed them (Lk. 9 :34). When Jesus left His disciples and returned to heaven, a cloud received Him out of their sight (Acts 1:9). Clouds, therefore, mark the glorious presence of God.

2. The rainbow upon his head (Rev. 10:1)

We have already seen the rainbow in chapter 4:3, surrounding the throne of God. In Genesis 9:11-17, the rainbow is given to mankind as the sign of a covenant, a promise that God made with mankind that He would never again destroy the earth with a flood. It is the symbol of God's mercy to humanity. In a vision, Ezekiel saw the rainbow surrounding the one with the appearance of a man, sitting on the throne in heaven, and he comments, "Such was the appearance of the likeness of the glory of the Lord" (Ez. 1:26-28). I believe this is the same one we are seeing in Revelation 10. He bears the rainbow of God's covenant of mercy because He is Mercy Incarnate, the One through whom all God's mercy flows. He is Jesus.

3. His face was like the sun (Rev. 12.1)

Already in Revelation we have seen this face (Rev. 1:16). It is the face of the risen and glorified Lord, shining in all its brilliance! It is the face that Peter, James, and John saw on the Mount of Transfiguration. It is the face of the One who dazzled Ezekiel by the river Chebar, whose glory lighted the earth (Ez. 43:2-3). Some refer to the angel in Rev. 18:1 who "lights up the earth with his glory" as being only an angel. It is my understanding that this, also, is Jesus, the Angel of the Lord, the great prophet of God, delivering a final message of doom to a sin-darkened world. No angel's face will ever shine like His glorious face!

4. His feet like pillars of fire (Rev. 10:1)

Once again we refer back to chapter one where we find the fullest description of Christ, a sure guide for identifying Him elsewhere. In verse 15 it says, "His feet were like burnished bronze when it has been caused to glow in a furnace". Again, in Ezekiel 1:27, it says of the

Lord of Glory, "and from the appearance of His loins and downward I saw something like fire". In Ezekiel 43:7, the Lord says to Ezekiel concerning the temple, "Son of man, this is the place of My throne, and the place of the soles of My feet". Note the prominence given to the two pillars that flanked the main door of Solomon's temple (I Kings 7:15-22). They were about thirty-five feet high and cast in bronze. In the light of sunrise, they must have shone as if on fire. It was as if the Lord was planting his feet at the place of His throne. In addition, the glory cloud that sat over the tabernacle became a pillar of fire by night (Ex 13:21), a symbol of the Lord standing guard over His people. The fire and the bronze are both symbols of judgment. The message of judgment conveyed by His fiery bronze feet is balanced by the rainbow of mercy about His head.

What he says

1. "He cried out with a loud voice, as when a lion roars" (Rev. 10:3)

The prophets spoke of a day when a lion would roar. "As the lion growls, ...so will the Lord of Hosts come down to wage war on Mount Zion and on its hill" (Is.31:4). "They will walk after the Lord; He will roar like a lion" (Hos. 11:10). "And the Lord roars from Zion and utters His voice from Jerusalem" (Joel 3:16). In each case it is the Messiah. In Revelation 5:5, He is called the Lion of the tribe of Judah. "When He had cried out, the seven peels of thunder uttered their voices" (Rev. 10:3). This is the only message of Revelation that is not revealed to us. In Psalm 29, there is a seven-fold reference to the voice of the Lord. It is a description of a violent thunderstorm. It is of note that the appearances of the glory of the Lord in Revelation are occasions of such storms (Rev. 4:5; 8:5; 11:19; 16:18). My own impression is that these thunders are descriptive of the final storm of God's judgment on earth. But we will speak of that later.

2. "He lifted up his right hand to heaven and swore by Him who lives forever…" (Rev. 10:5-6)

Some commentators assert that because this angel refers to the externally existent One, The Creator, as another person, then he cannot be Jesus. However, the Lord Jesus gave his Father honour in such a way before (Lk.10:21; Jn.10:29). We should not be surprised that the Son ascribes deity to the Father here and swears by His name.

There is a direct reference in Daniel 12:7 to one who swore in such a way concerning a prophetic time period. He is referred to as the "man dressed in linen who was above the waters of the river". We need to find out who this man is. In Daniel 8:16, he appears once again over the water between the banks of the Ulai and he instructs Gabriel to give Daniel an understanding of the vision. He appears again in Daniel 10 when Daniel was on the bank of the Tigris River. Verse six describes this glorious person; face like lightning, eyes like flaming torches, arms and feet like the gleam of bronze and the sound of his words like the sound of a tumult. This description fits well with Ezekiel 1 and Revelation 1, and I believe that this One is the Lord himself. From verse 10, as in the discourse of chapter eight, the actual disclosure to Daniel is given by an angel, most likely Gabriel. So, there is nothing here that discredits our understanding that the angel in Revelation 10 is the Lord himself.

What he does- He brings the little book

The Lord is bringing from heaven a little book for John to read. In order to understand the meaning of this whole scene we must know what the little book contains. I believe that the little book is the sum of Old Testament prophecy for the following reasons:

1. "He had in his hand a little book which was open" (Rev. 10:2)

This book is to be compared with the seven-sealed scroll of chapter five, because in both instances Christ is holding the book. Some may question why the book is described as little. I believe the book appears as small only because the angel is appearing as a colossus, His feet spanning land and sea. We saw in chapter 5 that the scroll is the sum of Old Testament prophecy. However, now the book is no longer sealed up, but rather is OPEN. If there is one thing that God wants us to read and note, it is His Word. God has freely given it to us. He has not hidden His thoughts but has expressed them in a book. This book does not contain dark mysteries, but instead brings light. It is opened!

Satan delights in hiding the truth from people. He is the master deceiver who deals in the occult (hidden things). In chapter eighteen, the religion of Babylon, which will be so popular in the last days, emphasizes mysteries which only the initiated will be able to understand (Rev. 2:24). The false religions of today, which are leading up to that final apostasy, have their secrets and their mysteries, but God is honest and straightforward. There is no Plan B, no hidden agenda, no fine print. God does not invite us to a blind or mindless faith. God's book is opened!

2. "Take it and eat it, and it will make your stomach bitter, but in your mouth, it will be as sweet as honey" (Rev. 10:9)

Another big clue to the nature of the little book is this description of its effect on John. Ezekiel had a similar experience when he received a scroll from the Lord (Ez. 2:8-3:4). We have already referred to the One giving the scroll being like the angel of Revelation 10 in His appearance. Now his action in relation to Ezekiel is exactly what happens to John. Ezekiel records that it was as sweet as honey in his mouth. The sweetness was the promise of God's mercy and grace. However, the message was also full of bitterness because it contained "lamentations, mourning, and woe" indicating God's judgment. That this message was the sum of all the prophetic messages that Ezekiel received from the Lord is clear. "Take into your heart all my words which shall speak to you and listen closely. And go to the exiles, the sons of your people, speak to them and tell them...(Ez. 3:10-11). Jeremiah describes a similar experience on receiving his message from the Lord (Jer. 1:9; 15:16). Now it is John's turn.

3. "You must prophesy again" (10:11)

When this statement is matched with the words of verse 7, the word AGAIN takes on great importance. What the Lord is saying is, "John, take the message that my people have heard already through my servants like Ezekiel and Jeremiah, and give it to them again. They did not listen the first time and fell into judgment. Now the time has come for all that has been written to come to pass. "John, give it to them again!" And so, as will soon be appreciated, nothing of these middle chapters of Revelation may be said to be new material, rather it is a gathering together of all that has been said already in the Old Testament prophecy.

The Holy Spirit is the great teacher and knows well the value of repetition. It is well known that the law was given twice to Israel, once at Mount Sinai through Moses, and again by Moses at the end of his life, just as the children of Israel were about to enter the promised land. This second giving of the law is found in Deuteronomy, which name means "the second giving of the law". Therefore, it should not surprise us that there should be a second giving of prophecy as well. The book of Revelation may be seen, then, as the DEUTERONOMY of Bible prophecy. Jesus is saying "Prophesy again!".

4. "Concerning many peoples and nations and tongues and kings"(Rev.10:11)

This takes up the Old Testament theme of Israel and the nations. The church today is 'a holy nation' (I Pet. 2:9), but not an earthly nation, because ' our citizenship is in heaven' (Phil. 3:20). The New Testament does not concern itself primarily with peoples and nations and tongues and kings because the church is 'all one in Christ Jesus' (Gal. 3:28). However, when the church is safely home in heaven, then God turns to the unfinished business of the kingdoms of this world, and the fulfilment of his promises to Israel. If the centrality of the earthly nation of Israel is not appreciated, then the interpretation of what follows in Revelation ends in hopeless confusion.

This, then, is the substance of the little book.

The Tabernacle Connection: The Candlestick.

The tabernacle was a symbol of God's light and glory shining out. Light is a symbol of truth. We still use this symbol in modern English. For instance, when someone learns some new truth, we say we have been enlightened. In the Holy Place there was a golden lampstand with seven lamps (Ex.37:17-24).   It was the job of the priests to daily trim its wicks and supply it with oil so that the light never went out. It continually bathed the Holy Place in a warm glow.It was the inner witness to the light of God's presence. Jesus is the lampstand. He said of Himself, "I am the light of the world" (John 8:12). He is the glorious outshining of all that the true God is. Jesus is the light in several ways:

1. His personal character is light.

The strong angel of Revelation 10 is an angel of light; clothed with a cloud, rainbow upon His head, face like the sun, feet like pillars of fire. All this speaks of heavenly light and glory. The writer of the book of Hebrews says the Son is "the radiance of His glory, and the exact representation of His nature" (Heb. 1:3). When Phillip asked Jesus to show the disciples the Father, Jesus answered, "He who has seen Me has seen the Father" (John 14:9). The witness of the apostle John concerning Jesus was, "We beheld His glory, glory as of the only begotten from the Father, full of grace and truth" (John 1:14). The reason Jesus looked like God is because He is God revealed in human flesh. John also said, "In the beginning was the Word, and the Word was with God and the Word was God" (John 1:1).

2. His prophetic work is to bring light.

The angel of Revelation chapter ten is serving in the role of a messenger bringing the little book to John. As such, He is a communicator of truth, a prophet. Moses prophesied concerning the Messiah that He would be "a prophet like unto me" (Deut. 18:15). Isaiah prophesied that those who saw the coming of the Messiah would experience a great light (Is. 9:2). The woman Jesus met at Jacob's well said, "I know that Messiah is coming...when that one comes he will declare all things to us" (John 4:25). When the people saw Jesus feed the 5000 people with five loaves and two fish, they said, "This is of a truth the prophet who is to come into the world" (John 6:14). All through John's gospel Jesus prefaces his words with, "Truly, truly", emphasizing their revelatory character. His witness was, "For I did not speak on my own initiative, but the Father Himself who sent me has given me commandment, what to say and what to speak" (John 12:49).

The inspired writer of Hebrews declares, "God, after He spoke long ago to the fathers in the prophets in many portions and in many ways, in these last days has spoken to us in His Son" (Heb. 1:1-2). Jesus is called "the Apostle and High Priest of our confession" (Heb. 3:1), emphasizing first His prophetic ministry, then His priestly ministry.

The personal character of the Lord Jesus and His prophetic work, then, are symbolized by the glorious Angel of Revelation 10. Jesus is that Angel. He is the Lampstand.

You are the light of the world

This scene of Jesus bringing the book to John indicates His ministry of equipping us, His church, to be the light as well. In this present age it is the church which is to be the light of the world. (Matt.5:14) Just as John was instructed to go and take the scroll from the hand of the angel, so we, too, are encouraged to receive the word which is able to save our souls (Ja.1:21). Just as John was instructed to feed on the word, we also are called to do so (Col. 3:17. Just as John was called to prophesy again, so we also are called to preach the word to all(IITim.4:2).

The darkness is increasing all around us. Satan is busy blinding the eyes of the unbelieving, that they may not see the light of the gospel of the glory of Christ, who is the image of God (II Cor. 4:4). Paul therefore encourages us to be busy, "by the manifestation of truth commending ourselves to every man's conscience in the sight of God" (II Cor. 4:2). We are the light of the world! Let's shine now for Jesus!

The Zechariah Connection

In Revelation 11:4, two prophets of God are described as being two lampstands. This reference is taken from Zechariah 4:14, and describes the work of Zerubbabel and Joshua in restoring the temple worship in their day. They bore faithful witness to the Lord (light symbolizing their witness) in the power of the Holy Spirit (symbolized by the oil). Similarly, two prophets of God will bear witness and prophesy in a coming day, in a spectacular display of the Spirit's power. These two prophets will be the true source of light in a dark world and point people to God in the coming day.

Another Tabernacle Connection

It is of interest to note that there was not one, but ten lampstands in Solomon's temple (II Chron. 4:7). Correspondingly, there are ten lampstands mentioned in Revelation. There are seven in chapter one, which represent the seven churches, each being a witness for Christ in this age, and now two in chapter eleven, which represents the prophetic witness in the tribulation. In the Millennial age, there will be but one lampstand, for Revelation 21:23 says, "And the city has no need of the sun or the moon to shine upon it, for the glory of God has illuminated it, and its lamp is the Lamb". Jesus is the eternal Lampstand!

1 and 2. The two witnesses 11:1-14

The first two characters in our drama are two mysterious witnesses. The opening verses of chapter 11 give us the time and place of their prophesying. John is told to measure the temple of God in the holy city. Such measuring took place in the Old Testament and was a sign of blessing (Ez. 40:3). Therefore, a temple will again stand on the mount in Jerusalem, the holy city, and worship will be carried on there. That is not the case today, because the Roman general Titus destroyed the temple of Christ's day in A.D. 70, and it has never been rebuilt. But the prophecies concerning the end of the age in Matthew's gospel indicate that a temple will be rebuilt on the temple mount in Jerusalem during the tribulation period (Matt. 24:15). This in itself will be a great rallying point for those Jews who are longing for such a holy place. However, it will be a mixed blessing, because at the same time they have gained some degree of spiritual freedom, they will also have lost some political freedom. It says that the court outside the temple, which is taken to mean the whole city of Jerusalem, will be trodden down by the Gentile powers. (According to Alfred Edersheim, in his book, The Temple, it states that during feast times, the court of the temple was expanded to include the whole city of Jerusalem.)Today the Jews have the city, but not the temple. According to these verses, in the future they will have the temple but lose control of the city to Gentile powers!

How will this state of affairs come to be? Scripture indicates that, in a coming day, there will be a seven-year peace treaty made between the nation of Israel and a strong Gentile power (Dan. 9:27). For the first three and a half years the Jews will be able to enjoy religious freedom, but at what cost? It appears that this religious freedom will be bought at the cost of relinquishing political control of Jerusalem. Perhaps the city will come under United Nations control for the first three and a half years of this treaty. It is during this time of religious freedom, but political compromise, that two prophets of God appear on the streets of Jerusalem. These two faithful men of God will be martyred on those same streets. Verse eight states that "their dead bodies will lie in the streets of the great city…, where also their Lord was crucified."

The Men and their Message

The two mystical names for Jerusalem in verse eight are very instructive. Sodom was a center for the worship of Baal and Ashtaroth, the leading gods in Canaanite religion, in whose temples the people practiced every form of sexual sin. Sodom, therefore, speaks of religious seduction. Egypt was one of the world's great empires, whose gods (like the sun god, Ra) symbolized power and glory. Egypt, therefore, speaks mystically of political seduction. It was Elijah who appeared before the prophets of Baal and Ashtoreth on Mount Carmel to defeat the prophets of Jezebel and break the religious seduction of these Canaanite gods.

It was Moses who appeared before Pharoah and his magicians to break the power of Egypt and the political seduction of Israel to those gods who are not gods.

It will be the opposition to the religious and political seduction of Israel by the preaching of the truth of God that occasions the appearing of these two latter day prophets.

These two men, physically clothed in sackcloth, which indicates a personal sense of mourning and repentance (Jonah 3:5-6), but spiritually clothed with power from on high, will play a major role in world politics. Who are they? I believe that the answer, as always, comes from reference to the Old Testament, where we are able to trace the following clues:

1. Their miracles

A. "They have the power to shut up the sky in order that the rain may not fall during the days of their prophesying" (11:6). Only one person in scripture performed this miracle, Elijah, the Tishbite (I Kings 17:1; James 5:17; Luke 4:25). Notice that it was the same time frame, three and a half years.

b. "They have power over the waters to turn them into blood and to smite the earth with every plague, as often as they desire" (11:6). Only one person in scripture did such a miracle, Moses, as he dueled with Pharoah of Egypt (Ex. 7:19).

Again note the divine protection afforded these two prophets. "Fire proceeds out of their mouth and devours their enemies". In the case of both Moses and Elijah, God, both protected them from their enemies and vindicated their ministry by fire from heaven (Num. 26:9-10; II Kings 1:10).

B. Their mysterious passing

Moses is the only person that God himself buried (Deut. 34:6), and that in a secret grave. In Jude 9, it is recorded that "Michael, the archangel, disputed with the devil, and argued about the body of Moses". For some reason the devil wanted to rob this grave. Elijah is one of only two people in the Old Testament that did not experience death, with his dramatic transport to heaven (II King2). This leads one to suspect that God is not finished with these two faithful men, Moses and Elijah.

C. Their mention in prophecy

The last two names in the Old Testament are Moses and Elijah (Mal. 4:4-6). Although it is not stated of Moses that he will return, it is specifically stated that Elijah the prophet would be sent by God in the end times.

D. Their appearance at the Transfiguration

They not only appeared with Christ on this occasion, but they also were speaking of Christ's soon-coming death at Jerusalem (Lk. 9:30-31). It would be possible then, that Moses and Elijah will actually be back on this earth to minister to Israel in their hour of great need, and to bear witness to the truth of God. They have been ideally prepared for the job. Some might object to the idea that Moses will return from being with the Lord because "it is appointed unto man once to die" (Heb.9:27). However, the Lord brought Lazarus back to life, and Peter, by the Spirit, brought Dorcas back to life. Following this, they each had a ministry before dying a second time, so we understand that "with God all things are possible".

Reaction to their Ministry

These two prophets will be met with much resistance and opposition. However, as verse seven makes clear, they will not suffer martyrdom until their testimony is finished. Notice it does not say that their enemies cut short their ministry. Rather, the One who has all things in His control allows His servants to experience death after they have finished all that was required of them.

The beast from the abyss who is responsible for the

prophets' demise is most likely the same beast who makes his appearance in chapter 13:1. He is a coming political leader called the antichrist. The watching world of "peoples, tribes, tongues, and nations" will give their glad assent to this violent act against God's servants. No doubt most regarded these two as troublemakers of the worst kind. Certainly, the conservationists would be against them for withholding the rain! But most of all, their message of calling people to repentance would gall the unbelieving of this world. With rejoicing and the exchange of gifts (shades of a perverted Christmas spirit), the enemies of God the world over watch the unburied corpses of God's witnesses for three and a half days. Then the unthinkable happens. Their corpses suddenly stir to life again! After hearing the call of the Lord to "Come up here!" (Rev.11:12), they stand to their feet, and before the incredulous and fearful hearts of their enemies, they ascend bodily into heaven. An earthquake follows, with devastation of part of the city and seven thousand lives are lost, leaving many terror-stricken and giving glory to the God of heaven.

God's Principle of Multiplication

In Mark 6:7-13 and 30-32, there is recorded the commissioning of the twelve apostles, and the record of the successful completion of their first mission. Sandwiched between these verses is the record of the martyrdom of John the Baptist at the hand of Herod. I believe these two episodes are inseparably connected. John, the great prophet of the kingdom and "the voice of (only) one crying in the wilderness" (Mark 1:3) had to die before the greater voice of the twelve apostles could be heard. John's testimony and sacrifice was the trigger. In Acts 1:8, just before Jesus ascends into heaven, He promises the Spirit to his own, and commissions them to be his witnesses. What was once the testimony of One becomes the united voice of millions by the power of the Spirit. Jesus had to die and then be glorified before that Spirit could be given and that testimony commence (John 7:39).

In like manner, the death and resurrection of these two Jewish prophets of the kingdom will be the spark, the ignition, the initiation, of a great multiplication of witnesses in this world. Ezekiel 1:37 describes how God revives the nation of Israel in a coming day. They are likened to a heap of bones in a valley. God says to them, "Behold I will cause breath to enter that you may come to life" (37:5). Just as God breathes the breath of life into the two witnesses of Revelation chapter eleven, in like manner he will spiritually restore the nation of Israel.

3. The Woman with the Child (Rev. 12:6)

If seeing the centrality of Christ in Revelation is the

first key to understanding the book, then the second key is seeing the physical nation of Israel as central in the prophecy. I believe that the woman here represented is the nation of Israel, and the male child is Christ. Others identify this woman as Mary, the physical mother of Christ. However, the Bible nowhere states that Mary will be crowned in heaven, nor does it describe a war between Mary and the dragon which answers to the details of verses 13-17. Still others see the woman as representing the church. However, it could never be said that the church bore Christ.

Once again, the Old Testament comes to our aid in making a positive identification here. In Gen 37:9-11, Joseph has a dream that the sun, moon, and eleven stars bowed down to him. He relates the dream to his brothers and to his father, Jacob, who then interprets the dream.

The sun is Jacob himself, the moon is Rachel, and the eleven stars are Joseph's brothers (Joseph being the twelfth star). The same twelve brethren are named for us in Revelation 7:4-8. Therefore, the clothing of the woman in Revelation 12 represents the physical nation of Israel.

Who, then, is the woman? She is stated to be a "great sign in heaven". The great prophet Isaiah gives us the answer. He repeatedly refers to Jerusalem in the feminine gender, calling her "the daughter of Zion" and Jesus also refers to her by the same name (Matt. 21:5). In Isaiah 1:21, Jerusalem, the faithful city has become a harlot, she who was full of justice". But in chapter 40 God says, "Speak kindly to Jerusalem; and call out to her that her warfare has ended, that her iniquity has been removed..." Again, in the closing chapters of the book of Isaiah, Jerusalem is the center of the affections of Jehovah (Is. 65:18-19; 66:10). This theme of the city of Jerusalem being the woman loved by Jehovah carries through other Old Testament prophets as well. In Ezekiel 16:32, Jerusalem is called the "adulteress wife", but the climax of the book is the building of the temple in Jerusalem and the name of the city from that day shall be, "The Lord is there" (Ez. 48:35). Of all the cities in the world, Jerusalem will wear the crown (Ps. 48).

Having established that the woman is Jerusalem, which, as the capital, represents the nation of Israel, the details following in Revelation 12 become clear. The labour and birth of verse 2 is that of Christ, the Messiah. The opposition of the dragon in verse 3 represents the attempt of Satan, through the treachery of King Herod (Matt. 2:13-21), to kill the Messiah. Immediately, in verse 5, "the child is caught up to God and his throne", signifying the ascension of Christ after His work on earth was completed. It may appear strange to some that the key elements of Christ's life, his death and resurrection are passed over without a word here. However, it is not Christ who is the central person of this passage, but rather, the woman who bore him. Christ appears only in a cameo role here. The next item of information skips over an even greater amount of history, for the escape of the woman and her divine protection is yet to be accomplished in a future day.

4. Michael

In Revelation 12:7, Michael, and his angels wage war with the dragon in heaven. Michael is called the archangel in Jude 9. In Daniel 12:1, he is referred to as "the great prince who stands guard over the sons of your (Daniel's) people." It is likely, then, that Michael is the guardian angel of Israel. The book of Daniel makes clear that behind the earthly scene of man's wars and political struggles there is a great spiritual struggle going on amongst the principalities and powers in heavenly places (Dan.10:10-21). The central struggle of all is that which bears on the nation of Israel. Michael and his hosts, then, make war with Satan and they prevail. Satan is thrown down to earth, and his minions are thrown down with him.

5. The Dragon

Satan (meaning 'adversary') appears early on the scene of man's history. He takes the form of a serpent and appears personally to Eve in the garden of Eden. His disguise is perfect, and Eve is totally deceived by the craft of Satan. Adam becomes an accomplice in the evil act, and sin and death become the lot of mankind. But the first prophecy in the Bible gives warning to Satan that the battle is not done. "The seed of the woman will bruise the serpent's head" (Gen. 3:15). The decisive battle where this is accomplished is the cross of Christ, where Jesus, the seed of the woman, destroys the works of the devil (IJohn 3:8).

However, by God's sovereign plan, he allows an opposition party to exist in the universe. Satan remains with entrance both to heaven and earth to promote his evil empire. As he appeared in the courts of heaven in Job's day (Job 1:6), so the devil (which means 'slanderer') continues to appear in order to "accuse the brethren" (Rev. 12:10). He also has access to this world where he is busy "deceiving the whole earth" (Rev. 12:10).

In a soon coming day, Michael and the angelic hosts will arise and cast Satan and his followers out of heaven to the earth. This is what is referred to in chapter 12:4

where the dragon's tail "swept away a third of the stars of heaven and threw them to earth". Heaven is thus cleared of his influence, but earth gets a double dose of his venom. The serpent is cornered and angry, and realizes his time is short. Daniel 12:1 says that when Michael arises "there will be a time of distress such as never occurred since there was a nation until that time". What follows is the fulfillment of that prophecy.

The key target of the dragon is the woman, that is, Jerusalem, and the nation of Israel. The two wings of the great eagle mentioned in verse 14 is an Old Testament symbol for God's protecting care (Ex. 19:4; Deut. 32:11). Notice the imagery of these verses. "The serpent poured water like a river out of his mouth after the woman that he might cause her to be swept away". It is possible that this is a literal river, but it more likely, that it is symbolic of some trial or judgment that the serpent brings to bear on the Jews. Seeing that this whole passage has to do with the prophets and their messages, I believe that what we are seeing here is a flood of EVIL PROPAGANDA to try to deceive even the very elect. Such imagery is common, note Revelation 11:5, where literal fire may not be meant, but rather judgment. Observe again in Revelation 19:15, where Christ Himself has a sharp sword coming out of His mouth (indicating judgment once again). However, God supernaturally nourishes and protects His own people in the wilderness. The vitriol and lies of Satan sink harmlessly into the sand.

6. The First Beast

The dragon is frustrated because he is not able to defeat the woman, so he goes off to make war with the rest of her children. If the woman is Jerusalem, then the rest of her children are those Jews living in different parts of the world who keep the commandments of God and hold to the testimony of Jesus. His frontal attack on the woman has already been foiled, so, for this battle he reverts to his ancient tactic of disguise. He stands on the seashore and up from the sea comes a most amazing beast. That this beast is not a phantasmal monster, but rather a man, is made clear from the text. Several points of description will clarify who he is, and what he does.

A. "Out of the Sea"(Rev.13:1)

When contrasted to "out of the earth" in verse 11, we are led to believe that this is a symbolic designation, as in Revelation 17:15, where the water refers to the variety of Gentile nations. However, more conclusive evidence comes from Daniel 7, from a vision of Daniel. There he sees four great beasts coming up out of the sea. The first three were like a lion, a bear and a leopard. The fourth beast's appearance was far more terrifying than the other beasts. This beast was to be the "kingdom which would devour the whole earth" (7:23). This beast is like Rome, the fourth Gentile power mentioned in Daniel, that subdues Israel in the time of Christ. Verse 24 goes on to say that out of this kingdom ten kings will arise. These ten kings will form the backbone of the political power base of the beast of Revelation. They will be Gentle nations.

B. "Having ten horns and seven heads…" (Rev.13:1)

…and on his horns were ten diadems, and on his heads were blasphemous names" This description is very similar to that of the dragon in 12:3, and the relationship is further cemented when we read that the dragon gave him his power and his throne and great authority. The number of horns and heads speak of combined power, a political union. Daniel 9:26 leads us to believe that this political leader is to be European, because the "people of the prince who is to come will destroy the city". We know that the city of Jerusalem was destroyed by the Roman army, that is, Europeans. The multiplicity of horns and heads may indicate a union of nations. Whatever political union it may be, it gives all power and authority to the beast.

C. "I saw one of its heads as if it had been slain, and his fatal wound was healed" (Rev.13:3)

It appears that the greatness of this person called the beast will undergo some test, perhaps an attempted assassination, as we have commonly seen among world leaders. However, what appears to be sure death ends up in a dramatic escape from death. Many will take this as a sign of omnipotence and will worship the dragon for giving him such power.

D. "a mouth speaking arrogant words and blasphemies."(Rev.13:5)

This man's mouth is under the authority of Satan. His arrogance will lead him to declare himself as worthy of worship of all men, and his blasphemy will be to force men to worship him. Concerning him, the apostle Paul declares "the man of lawlessness..., the son of destruction, who opposes and exalts himself above every so-called god or object of worship, so that he takes his seat in the temple of God, displaying himself as being God" (II Thess. 2:3-4).

E. "Authority to act for forty-two months was given to him" (Rev.13:5)

II Thessalonians 2: 6-7 tells us that this beast will not make his appearance on the stage of world history until the restrainer is taken out of the way. This restrainer would appear to be the Holy Spirit resident in the church today. Therefore, when the church is called to heaven, the beast will begin to make his presence felt in the world. It appears that he will first perform a great political feat by bringing peace to the Middle East. What the Jews give up is the control of the city of Jerusalem (Rev. 11:2) but what they receive is a guarantee peace with their neighbors and permission to build their temple on the temple mount.

The first three and a half years of this treaty will see various troubles in the world, especially for those who believe in Jesus, but the majority of Jews will be unaffected. They will be in awe of this Gentile for giving them peace, for delivering them out of the hands of their enemies. They will no doubt think of him as their modern-day Moses! Then at the close of this time of relative peace, the two prophets of God will be killed in Jerusalem. Following this, the beast will "put a stop to sacrifice and grain offering" (Dan. 9:27) and erect his idol in the Holy Place (Matt. 24:15). The three and a half years following this act of blasphemy, when the beast will have total control of the world, will mark the worst atrocities, the worst bloodshed, and the worst disasters that this world has ever seen! (Matt.24:21)

7. The Second beast (Rev.13:11)

Just as the Lord has had his two prophets, the dragon has his two beasts. He calls up the second beast from the earth. What are characteristics of this man?

A. "Out of the earth"

If the sea represents the Gentile nations, then the earth represents the Holy Land, the land that God promised long ago to Abraham and to his children. That makes this beast a Jew. Another tip off to the Jewishness of this man is a prophecy in Daniel 11:37. The context of this chapter is the invasion of Antiochus Epiphanes, a Syrian king who, in 167 BC, desecrated the temple in Jerusalem and set up an idol in the Holy Place. However, by the time we reach verse 36 of Daniel 11, the prophecy reaches on to the end times, and the coming of the one who will, like Antiochus, desecrate the temple. Verse 37 states that "he will show no regard for the god of his fathers or for the desire of women". These thoughts are distinctively Jewish, since the God of the fathers was the God of Abraham, Issac, and Jacob. The desire of women was the hope of all godly Jewish women to bear the Messiah. This man being referred to, then, is not Antiochus, but rather a man of a coming day who would erect such an idol in the temple. And that man is a Jew.

B. "He had two horns like a lamb, and he spoke as a dragon" (Rev.13:11)

Here is the original wolf in sheep's clothing! His outward appearance is that of a lamb. That means that he will in many ways look like Jesus, the Lamb of God. However, Jesus spoke with the authority of his Father, this man will speak with the authority of Satan.

C. "He exercises all the authority of the first beast in his presence" (Rev.13:12)

Once again, the issue of authority comes to the fore. Just as Christ did not claim to speak on His own authority, so this man speaks as an agent of another. As Christ's work was to direct the worship of men to the Father (Matt. 6:9), so this man's work will be to make the earth and those who dwell therein to worship the first beast. To that end, he performs great signs and wonders as proof of his statements. He makes fire come down out of heaven to earth in the presence of men, thus imitating the miracle Elijah performed at Mount Carmel (1 Kings.18:38)

**D. "And he deceives those who dwell on the earth"
(Rev.13:14)**

The work of this false prophet is twofold.

First, he will instruct those who dwell on the earth, that
is the Jews, to make an image of the beast. This reminds
us of Aaron's great apostasy in creating the golden cow
for the Israelites to worship. The prophet Daniel tells
us of this image, called the abomination of desolation
(Dan, 9:27; 11:31), which, when set up in the temple in
Jerusalem, will be the sign of the beginning of the great
tribulation (Matt. 24:15-24). The second beast will force
all to worship this image, and failure to do so will result
in death, just as Nebuchadnezzar commanded concerning
his idol in Daniel's day (Dan. 3:1-6).

Second, he will decree that all will have to take the name
of the first beast on their foreheads or on their right hand,
failure to do so barring one from the privilege of buying or
selling. The number of this name is 666, which may be a
bar code under the skin. The Israelites were to have the
sign of Jehovah on their hand and on their forehead, "that
the law of the Lord may be in your mouth" (Ex. 13:9). The
name of the beast would supplant the name of Jehovah !

In summary, this evil prophet will lead the people of the land to break the first three of the ten commandment.

Commands of prophet	Commands of God
1. Worship the first beast (13:12)	1. No other gods before Me
2. Make an image to the beast (13:14)	2. No graven images.
3. Name of the beast on forehead (13:17)	3. God's name not to be taken in vain.

Victory in Jesus

The finale of the war of the prophets is pictured in chapter 14:1-5. The Lamb is celebrating His triumph with the 144,000 faithful ones of Israel, the ones we learned of in chapter 7. They are marked by the seal of the living God. As the followers of the beast bear his name on their foreheads, a symbol of the devotion of their minds and hearts to him, so the followers of the Lamb are blessed with His name, and the name of the Father, on their foreheads, a symbol of devotion to Him. They are also distinguished by their character in two ways:

1. "They have not been defiled with women, for they have kept themselves chaste" (Rev.14:4)

This may indicate a special call to service as indicated in Matthew 19:12 and I Corinthians 7:29-35, where the married state would compromise their ability to function for God with no distractions. However, the strong word 'defiled' suggests a sinful liaison, something which marriage is not. Perhaps what is being referred to here is the commitment of God's servants to avoid the polluting influence of Babylonian religion which involved worship by ritual prostitution (Rev. 17:2; 18:3-4).

2. "No lie was found in their mouth; they are blameless" (Rev 14:5)

Notice the emphasis on the word 'mouth' in this section (10:9-10; 11:5; 12:15-16; 13:2, 5, 6), denoting the power of the spoken word, for good or for evil. Evidently, these 144,000 have a ministry, most likely to be the vanguard in the greatest missionary movement the world would ever see. "And this gospel of the kingdom shall be preached in the whole world for a witness to all the nations, and then the end shall come" (Matt. 24:14). These will be the true Jehovah's witnesses! They will speak only the truth of God to a world inundated with a flood of Satanic lies.

Where they take their stand

This scene takes us into millennial glory where the Lamb has come to Mount Zion to establish His throne. This is in keeping with the center of action for this whole prophetic section, that is, the city of Jerusalem. As the section opens with the Lord, the great prophet, descending from heaven with an opened book, to stand in solidarity with his prophet John, so now He stands in triumph with His faithful ones, as an opened heaven provides musical accompaniment for their song. How fitting that, in that opening scene of this section of the book, He stands with His feet on land and sea. Soon would come a beast out of the sea and out of the land. The Lord, by His stance, is saying, "Come, you prophets of hell. I already know all about you. I gave you life and breath, and with them you speak lies and deception. But you will go no further. YOU ARE UNDER MY FEET! I will crush you at the appointed time because My word cannot be broken".

 At the close of it all, the enemies of the Lamb are not to be found on Mt. Zion. Their final destruction will be described in the following chapters.

Vision V

CHRIST

THE JUDGE

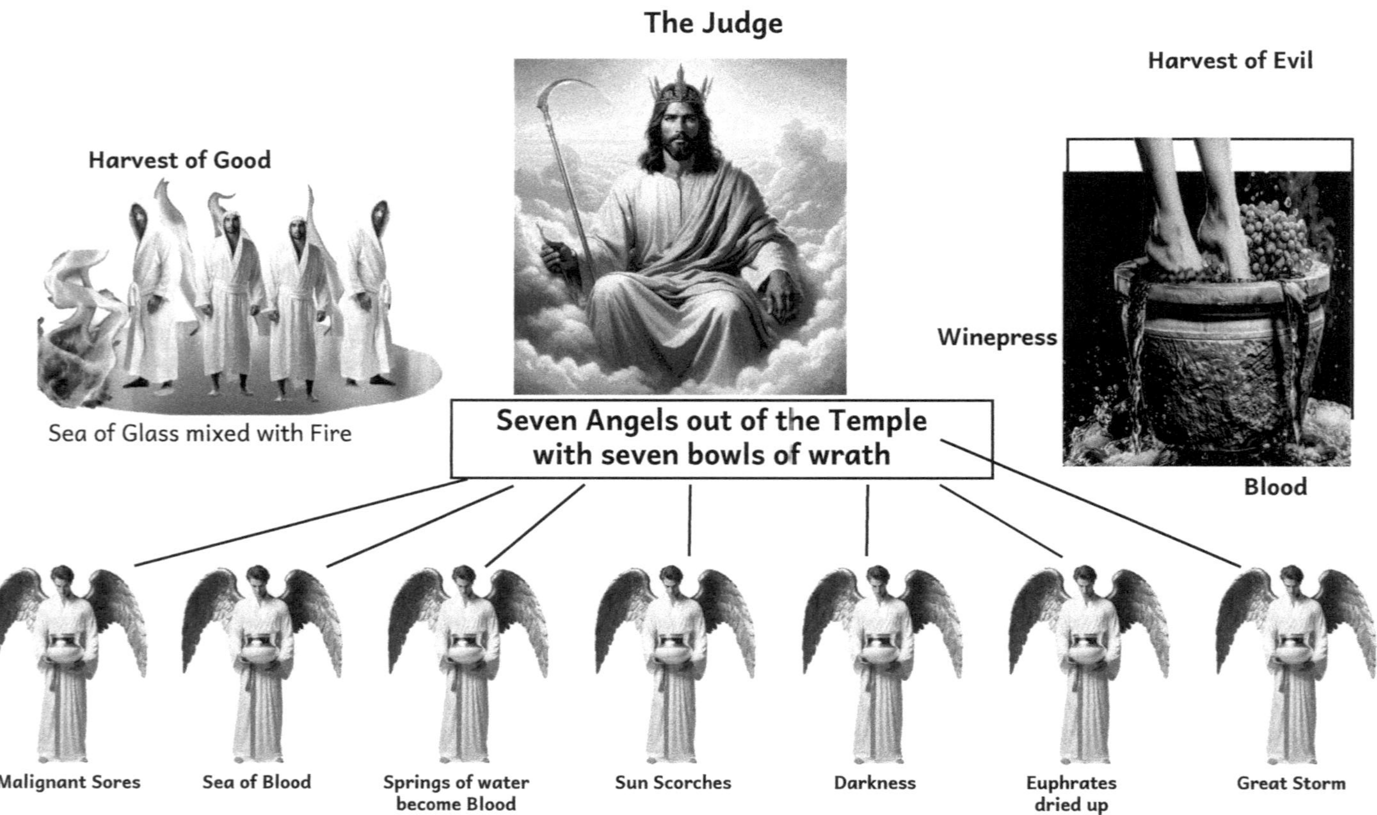
Harvest of Good
Sea of Glass mixed with Fire
The Judge
Harvest of Evil
Winepress
Blood
Seven Angels out of the Temple with seven bowls of wrath
Malignant Sores
Sea of Blood
Springs of water become Blood
Sun Scorches
Darkness
Euphrates dried up
Great Storm

Christ the Judge

To open this new section starting in Rev 14:6, three angels sent from God appear on the scene, flying above the earth. They bring an invitation, an announcement and a warning.

The invitation is to respond to the gospel of God's grace, to fear the One who alone is to be feared, and to worship the One who alone is worthy of our worship. This is the last offer of salvation to those who are still without a Saviour.

The announcement by the second angel is of the impending fall of the great city Babylon which is the center for all the political and religious opposition to the Lord.

The warning comes to those who choose to worship the beast rather than the living God. Here we see an important bit of imagery which will help to tie the whole section together under the theme of judgment. The wrath of God is linked to a cup of strong wine, and those judged by God are pictured as those drinking it. Coupled with this is the warning that the lake of fire awaits those who refuse the gospel.

That the message of the gospel goes out to those of every nation and tribe and tongue and people teaches the justice and equity of God. He will see to it that no one is unaware of the message that might save him or her. No one will be able to plead ignorance. Also, from the description of the lake of fire we see that those in it endure in some form of existence; their torment is experienced eternally, and their lack of rest is day and night. In blessed contrast to this horrible judgment is the rest and reward given to those who will suffer martyrdom for their faith during these last difficult days of this age.

Note that throughout this section two basic elements are used as symbols of judgment, one is water and the other is fire. In fact, all through the scriptures God uses these two media, water and fire to express his judgments (Num. 31:23; Is. 43:2; IPet.4:12; Ps. 69:14). Even in today's English these two symbols still speak of trial and disaster. We might refer to a flood of trouble or the fires of trial. Angels are the agents in these judgments, so we will be introduced to the angel who has power over fire (Rev. 14:18) , and the angel of the waters (Rev. 16:5). These two symbols of judgment come together in the final act of God's judgment, the lake of fire.

The Zechariah Connection

In chapter 5 of Zechariah, there are two visions which speak of judgment and cleansing, the vision of the flying scroll (5:1-4), and the vision of the woman in the ephah (5:5-11). Just as the three angels of Revelation 14 come flying in midheaven, so the principals in these two visions are seen to be flying. The idea in both instances would seem to be that the messages will be openly displayed, just as these days one might advertise an event by floating a banner behind a plane flying overhead. Both are flying over 'the land', which denotes the land of Israel. Thus, it is Israel that is to be cleansed.

The Flying Scroll

Several clues lead us to believe that the flying scroll stands for the Old Testament law embodied in the Ten Commandments.

First, in verse 3 it is called 'the curse'. When Israel affirmed three times before Moses and before God that they would keep the law (Ex. 19:8; 24:3,7), they inherited not only its blessings but also its curses (Deut. 27:26).

Second, the scroll is described as having a judgment against the one who swears on one side, and a judgment against the one who steals on the other side. This would accord with the Ten Commandments written on two

tablets of stone, where the middle commandment of the
first five (you shall not take the name of the Lord your
God in vain) represents sins directly against God, and the
middle commandment of the second five (you shall not
steal) represents sins against a neighbor.

Third, the judgment is reminiscent of the law of leprosy
which describes the complete destruction of a leprous
house (Lev. 14:45).

Fourth, the dimensions of the scroll are equal to the porch
of Solomon's temple (I Kings 6:3), a place where the book
of the law was normally read. The message here is that
the Lord, the righteous Judge is going to purge and purify
his people according to the righteous standard which they
pledged to keep.

The Ephah

The ephah, a basket slightly larger than a bushel, was
used for gathering in the grain harvest. The woman in the
ephah is specifically named "WICKEDNESS". The picture
is of a harvest of wickedness, typified here by a woman.
That is because the idolatrous practices of Babylon
were still fresh in the minds of the Israelites, who so
recently were captives there. The Babylonians worshipped
Semiramis (Rhea), the great goddess "mother", the

Queen of Heaven (Jer. 7:18), and her child Tammuz (Ez. 8:14). It is little wonder then, that the ephah should be transported to Shinar, which is the ancient name for Babylon and that a temple be made, and the woman installed upon a pedestal that she may be worshipped (Rev. 17:1-5; 18:7).

What is to be made of the two women upon whose wings the ephah is carried? The women are also associated with evil because they are pictured as storks, which are unclean birds. It so happens that there were two women of great influence for wickedness in Israel's history. The first was Queen Jezebel, who came to Israel as Ahab's wife, bringing with her the Sidonian gods, Asherah and Baal (I Kings 6:31-33), thus thoroughly establishing these idol gods in the northern kingdom. It is interesting that Alexander Hislop, in his classic text, "The Two Babylons", associates Asherah with Semiramis, and Baal with Tammuz. Notice also that the prophetess who was deceiving the church at Thyatira is called Jezebel (Rev. 2:20).

Jezebel's daughter, Athaliah, married into the royal line of the kings of Judah, and, by treachery, became queen for six years. During that time, idolatry flourished in the southern kingdom, and a temple was built for Baal right in Jerusalem (II Chron 23:17). Athaliah has the dubious distinction of being the only woman specifically called 'wicked' in the whole Bible (II Chron 24:7).

These two women, who almost completely corrupted Israel by encouraging the worship of the gods of Babylon, would ably qualify to set up such worship again. That the woman in the ephah is thrown back into the basket and then covered by a lid would indicate the cleansing of Israel, and the rejection of evil by at least some of its people.

But, since the ones who carry the basket away to Shinar are viewed as evil, it would speak of the fact that Jezebel and Athaliah's influence still causes many to practice idolatry. Their wicked fascination takes them in spirit back to Babylon, the land of bondage, to worship its goddess again, and perpetuate the idolatry of Israel. That is the main message of the corresponding chapters of Revelation. (Rev.14:8).

Court is in Session

In Revelation 14:14, another vision in the sky is now presented to John's eyes. There is a white cloud, and sitting on the cloud is one like a son of man, having a golden crown on his head, and a sharp sickle in his hand. It should be obvious that this is Jesus himself, but for sake of argument, let's go over the clues.

1. One like a "son of man" (Rev.14:14)

The first vision of Christ in Revelation identifies the Lord Jesus as a son of man (Rev. 1:13), and no one else in the book is given this description. There is a dramatic passage in Daniel 7:13 where one "like a son of man" appears before the court of heaven and receives dominion over all the peoples of all the nations. This mysterious One is none other than the Lord Jesus. The Father has given the Lord Jesus "authority to execute judgment, because He is the Son of Man" (John 5:27).

2. A white cloud (Rev.14:14)

In chapter 10, Christ appears clothed with a cloud. In Revelation 17 we are told, "Behold He is coming with clouds". You will remember that a cloud of glory rested over the tabernacle of God in the wilderness to mark His divine presence.

3. A sharp sickle (Rev.14:14)

The sickle is an instrument of harvest so well known in the farming economy of Israel. In Joel 3:13, the sickle becomes the instrument of judgment in the hand of the Lord. In verse 2 of the same chapter, the Lord says, "I will gather all the nations and bring them down to the valley of Jehoshaphat. Then I will enter into judgment with them there on behalf of My people." In verse 10, He invites the people to choose their own weapons, "Beat your plowshares into swords and your pruning hooks into spears". Then, in verse 12, the Lord says, "Let the nations be aroused and come up to the valley of Jehoshaphat, for there I will sit to judge all the surrounding nations. Put in the sickle for the harvest is ripe. Come, tread, for the winepress is full; the vats overflow for their wickedness is great. Multitudes, multitudes in the valley of decision! For the day of the Lord is near in the valley of decision." In this passage we find answers for our questions. Who is the one who wields the sickle? Surely, it is the Lord. What is He doing? He is judging the nations.

Notice the position of the judge, both in Joel and in Revelation. He is SITTING. It is interesting to note this is the first time that the Lord is pictured as sitting in Revelation. In chapter 1 He is standing in the middle of the lampstands. In chapter 5 He is a Lamb standing before the throne. In chapter 8 He stands at the golden altar, and in chapter 10 He stands with His right foot on the sea and His left foot on the land. Only now He sits. Why? Because when the judge sits, then the court is in session!

4. A golden crown (Rev.14:14)

Thus far in the book, Christ has not appeared wearing a crown, but in chapter 19 He is said to have many diadems on His head, for at that time He is coming as King of

Kings. What might be the reason for the crown in His role as judge? In the Old Testament the wisest judge was also a king, King Solomon. His most famous case is recorded in I Kings 3:16-28, where two women each laid claim to be the mother of one baby. By calling for a sword and threatening to divide the baby in half so that each could have a share, he was able to discern, by the reactions of the women, which was the rightful mother. Jesus said, "The Queen of the South shall rise up with this generation at the judgment and shall condemn it, because she came from the ends of the earth to hear the wisdom of Solomon, and behold, something greater than Solomon is here" (Matt. 12:42). Jesus is the JUDGE-KING, just like Solomon, but His wisdom far transcends that of Solomon. I am so glad that the judgment of this world is not left to a mere man, no matter how wise he may be. It is Jesus the all-knowing, all holy, all loving, the one crowned with glory and honor, who will speak the words which will forever seal the destiny of men. "Shall not the judge of all the earth deal justly?" (Gen.18:25).

The Two Harvests

It is my understanding that there are two harvests described here. The first one is accomplished by the Judge Himself in verse 16. The second is accomplished by the angel in verse 19. John the Baptist makes reference to the dual nature of the harvest in Matt.3:12, first a harvest of good followed by a harvest of evil. Notice how incongruous it is for the angel to harvest the grapes with a sickle. The goal is not to preserve the grapes but to completely destroy the vineyard!

It is the separating of things that differ that is the essence of judgment. The Lord said, "I will shake the house of Israel among all the nations as grain is shaken in a sieve, but not a kernel will fall to the ground. All the sinners of my people will die by the sword..." (Amos 9:9-10). None of the true seed will be lost in this judging process.

The Harvest of Good

As stated already, there is a symbolism that ties this whole section of the book together, that is, fire and water. In chapter fifteen, verse two, there are a group of people who appear in heaven, some translations say, "on a sea of glass mixed with fire", some say, "beside a sea of glass mixed with fire." This is undoubtedly the same glassy sea that we find mentioned in Revelation 4, which is before the throne of God, only here the element of fire is added.

They are described as victors, having successfully resisted the temptation to join with the antichrist. They are to be identified with the suffering saints of Revelation 14:13 and 12:11, who would rather die a martyr's death than deny their Lord. Now they have entered their rest and sing of the glories of the Almighty. But why are they pictured as being on (or, beside) the sea of glass mixed with fire? Once again, the Old Testament supplies the answer.

Surely the most renowned of all the victories God accomplished for Israel was their deliverance from Egypt. God did it in a way that proved His great power over the armies of Egypt, the greatest military force of the day. He also taught His own people a lesson of faith. He brought them to the edge of the Red Sea where they realized they were trapped between the water and the advancing armies of Pharoah. Then He told them to go forward (Ex. 14:15)! "Surely God is joking", Moses must have thought, "for if we go forward into the water, we shall die." Then God had Moses lift his rod over the expanse of the sea, and that great body of water parted to form a dry path to the other side.

The Red Sea was a place of judgment, for God used its waters to destroy the armies of Egypt that followed after the Israelites. But what appeared to be a place of judgment and death for the children of Israel now became the path to life! Then Moses and the children of Israel stood on the far shore and lifted up their voices in praise and thanksgiving to God. They sang the song of Moses (Rev. 15:3)!

Similarly, these martyrs of the tribulation stand by the glassy sea mixed with fire. They have experienced the fiery trials and have been faithful unto death. They have walked through the trials of earth and patiently endured. Now they stand in a place of judgment before the very throne of God, and they do not die, but they live! And they rejoice, singing "the song of Moses, the bondservant of God, and the song of the lamb"; the song of Moses because they are safely through the sea, and the song of the Lamb, because without the blood of the Passover Lamb they would never have even begun the journey to salvation.

The Tabernacle Connection: The Laver

In the court of the tabernacle, between the altar of sacrifice and the door of the tent, was the laver, a bowl fashioned of brass, where the priests performed the ceremonial washing of hands and feet before doing the service in the Holy Place (Ex. 30:17-21). In the temple of Solomon, the laver gave place to a much larger structure called a sea, cast from bronze, and supported by twelve bronze oxen. It was approximately forty-five feet in circumference and could hold about 17,000 gallons of water. It was surrounded by a series of ten smaller basins, which were used to cleanse things for the burnt offering, but the sea itself was reserved for the priests to wash in (II Chron 4:2-6). Besides this practical function, the sea, which was shaped like a lily blossom, added to the splendor of the temple façade by reflecting its glory in the crystal water.

The sea of glass before the throne of God in heaven is symbolized by the sea before the temple of Solomon. This was the same sea that Ezekiel saw in his vision. It is of great interest to compare Ezekiel's description of the glassy sea and its angelic foundations (Ez. 1:4-28) with the description of the design of the ten smaller basins which accompanied the sea of Solomon's temple (I Kings 7:27-39). Cherubim, lions, oxen, wheels, all undergirding these mini seas are undoubtedly meant to remind us that because God is holy and lives in utmost purity, those who would approach him must be cleansed and purified. "Righteousness and justice are the foundation of Thy throne" (Ps. 97:2).

The Principle of Cleansing

The practical teaching concerning the laver or the sea is rich throughout scripture. God required personal purity in those who would commune with Him and serve Him. "Who may ascend into the hill of the Lord? And who may stand in His holy place? He who has clean hands and a pure heart.." (Ps. 24:3-4).

It is true that the altar of sacrifice, speaking as it does of the one sacrifice for sins, proclaims that the blood of Jesus His Son, cleanses us from all sin" (I John 1:7). However, the Bible speaks of another cleansing which Christ provides for His people, "the washing of water with the word" (Eph. 5:26). The water speaks of judgment, not the kind of judgment that damns, but the kind of judgment that applies discipline so that the recipient will be corrected, instructed, cleansed and blessed. (Heb. 12:5-11). This judgment is "with the word", meaning "according to the principles laid down in the word of God" (Ps. 119:9).

Again, the altar of sacrifice speaks of the once-for-all cleansing from sin accomplished in the life of a believer when he puts his faith in the shed blood of Christ. The laver speaks of the daily cleansing of his life by the activity of the Holy Spirit, using the word of God. The Lord Jesus acted out a living parable of this truth with His disciples in John 13 when He washed their feet. When Peter resisted, most likely from embarrassment, Jesus said, "If I do not wash you, you will have no part with me". The idea of 'no part' means 'no fellowship'. Peter then said, "Not my feet only, but also my hands and my head". Then Jesus answered him, "He who has bathed has only to wash his feet, but is completely clean; and you are clean, but not all of you".

Two kinds of cleansing are again distinguished. The disciples were clean because they had trusted the Lord and were forgiven their sins. On this point, Judas was the only one not clean, because he certainly was not a believer. However, they all required the second cleansing, the washing of the feet, because they had dirtied their feet along the way. So too, the believer dirties his feet by sinning everyday, and needs to confess those sins and be cleansed by the Lord. Sometimes that cleansing is a painless process, only a 'little water', but other times it comes with pain and trouble, a flood of water, that we might the better learn to be clean.

In his first epistle, which so beautifully deals with the problem of why Christians suffer, Peter gives us another reason besides cleansing from our sin that would account for trials in our life. In the plan of God for us, we may be called upon to undergo suffering for righteousness' sake (I Pet 3:17). God uses even this suffering to "perfect, confirm, strengthen, and establish you" while calling you to "His eternal glory in Christ" (I Pet. 5:10). This is why Paul could say, "We exalt in our tribulations "(Rom. 5:3), because he knew that they were being used by God to eventually bless him (Ro. 8:17). That is why the Spirit says, "If indeed we suffer with Him, in order that we may be glorified with Him" (Ro. 8:17).

And when we have passed through this trial, we too stand on the other side of the sea of glass mixed with fire, a people purified by the waters of trial and the fires of affliction, now looking upon the face of the One on the throne, and, as surely as the water reflects His glory, so we too, having been transformed into His likeness, will reflect the glory of the Lord (II Cor. 3:18).

The One to whom we go for salvation is also the One to whom we go for cleansing. Jesus is the Laver!

The Harvest of Evil

The harvest of evil is pictured in two related activities so well known in the agrarian society of Israel: the making of the wine (II Chron 11:11) and the drinking of the wine. The first picture centers on a winepress, the second on a cup or bowl.

The Winepress (Rev.14:19)

The symbolism of the winepress draws many Old Testament scriptures together, giving a vivid and awesome description of the JUDGE at work.

The words of Rev. 14:20 are strikingly literal, as the prophet sees a river of blood, originating 'outside the city', with 'blood up to the horses' bridles' and 'for a distance of 200 miles'. The Old Testament offers an abundance of graphic detail concerning man's very literal appointment with the One who will "judge among the nations" (Ps. 110:6).

Outside the City (Rev.14:20)

The prophet Joel identifies the city of judgment as Jerusalem (Joel 3:16). He further describes the place as the valley of decision (3:14). This is not a place for men to decide about God, but for God to decide about men! The valley is also called Jehoshaphat, which means "Jehovah judges". In fact, Jehoshaphat was the king noted for the establishing a system of judges in Judah (II Chron 19:4-11). There is no valley of Jehoshaphat near Jerusalem, or in all of Israel, but the story of how Jehoshaphat defeated the invading Moabites and Ammonites (II Chron. 20), will afford us some clues as to where this valley might be. Completely outnumbered by the enemy, Jehoshaphat gathered all the people of Judah to pray and seek the Lord. He himself prayed, "O our God, wilt thou not judge them? For we are powerless…" God answered them through the prophets saying, "The battle is not yours, but God's", and then told them to go out(from Jerusalem) with singing and rejoicing to the ascent of Ziz, to the southeast of Jerusalem and near Engedi. When the Israelites got there, they looked down on the corpses of their enemies, whom God had destroyed supernaturally.

In Zechariah 14:4, we learn that when the Lord returns, His feet will touch down on the Mount of Olives, which is just to the east of Jerusalem, and "the Mount of Olives will be split in its middle from east to west by a very large valley". This valley created by the Lord for purposes of judgment would appear to be the 'valley of decision' and the 'valley of Jehoshaphat'.

Blood up to the Horses' Bridles (Rev.14:20)

This expression indicates a very large slaughter. In Jehoshaphat's victory, perhaps thousands were slain, but that carnage is insufficient for the expression we have here. When God supernaturally destroyed the army of Sennacherib, numbered at over 100,000, outside the gates of Jerusalem, blood flowed in greater measure, but for blood to reach the depth of greater than four feet, hundreds of millions would have to be involved. Revelation 19:18 describes those involved in this final destruction and states, "the flesh of horses and those who sit on them and the flesh of all men". It says ALL MEN would become the supper of the birds who would gather to consume the carrion.

In Luke 17:34-37, the Lord made a statement concerning his second coming and the judgment. "On that night there will be two men in one bed; one will be taken and the other will be left. There will be two women grinding at the same place; one will be taken and the other left". There is no hint of these people being at war; they are only men and women, sleeping by night and working by day. It appears that the angel who reaps the vine of the earth will not only gather the armies of men who rise up against Him at Jerusalem, but ALL UNBELIEVING MEN AND WOMEN the world over. Notice the Lord's inclusion of a day scene and a night scene, taking in different sides of the world. When the disciples asked where they would be taken, the Lord answered. "Where the body is, there also will the vultures be gathered". They will be brought to the valley of decision! Multitudes, multitudes in the valley of decision!

For a distance of two hundred miles (Rev.14:20)

We have already seen that the valley of decision would open in an easterly direction from Jerusalem through the Mount of Olives. From that height there is a steep descent to the Dead Sea, the lowest place on earth. Another Old

Testament reference shows us where the river of blood goes from there. Isaiah 63:1-6 is one of the most powerful and chilling scenes in the whole Bible. Before reading this reference, it is wise to first read Isaiah 53 which shows us the magnificent grace of the Saviour at His first coming, because Isaiah 63 pictures Him as the Judge at His second coming. Now we see Him treading the winepress alone. He who was trodden down at Calvary is treading all His foes beneath His feet!

Notice from where He comes. He comes from Edom, the ancient land of Esau south of the Dead Sea. Edom, which means 'red', is the name given to Esau after he carelessly gave up his birthright to his brother Jacob one day, in return for a pot of red stew (Gen. 25:29-34).

The judgment against the land of Edom is spelled out in Isaiah 34:1-8, where "the sword of the Lord descends for judgment upon Edom" and "their land will be soaked with blood". This description of the day of the Lord's vengeance far transcends any local judgment, for it says in verse 2, "The Lord's indignation is against all the nations, and His wrath against all their armies..." They are guilty as Esau was, in their careless rejection of God's mercy and unrelenting hatred of God's people. Notice verse 4, which is quoted in Revelation 7 as part of the events in the sixth seal. This is, therefore, not a judgment of long past, but one which waits for the Lord's return.

As Allen Beechick has pointed out in his book, The Pretribulation Rapture, "Edom is far from Jerusalem and the beginning of the river of blood, but not yet 200 miles distant. A further reference to judgment upon Edom in Jeremiah 49 speaks of a great earthquake, the effects of which reach down as far as the Red Sea (Jer. 49:21). That would be at Ezion-Geber, which is the present port city of Elath. The river of blood will finally flow into the Red Sea, making it red as its name, and linking it with the historic crossing of that same sea, where Egyptian blood once ran. Just as at the Red Sea, where God created a valley with walls of water as a path through the sea, the people of God will be saved by fleeing into it (Zech.14:5). But that same valley will be the scene of their enemy's destruction. This path for the river of blood is part of a natural fault line in the earth's crust which begins in the Jordon valley and continues south into the African continent as the Great Rift Valley. In Zechariah 14:4, an earthquake is implied, and this is most likely the quake mentioned in Revelation 16 which signals the final act of this world's judgment."

The Bowls and Cups

The second picture of the judgment of the wicked

is symbolized by the drinking of wine from a cup, or the spilling of it from a bowl. Babylon is pictured as a woman adorned in rich attire with a name written on her forehead, "Babylon the Great, the Mother of Harlots and of Abominations of the Earth" (Rev. 18:5). She is drinking from a gold cup (Rev. 17:4-6) which represents the measure of her many sins, three of which are highlighted. She was involved in the practice of abominations, meaning witchcraft (Rev. 17:4; 18:23), immorality (Rev. 14:8; 17:2, 4;18:3), and the murder of the saints of God, the red of the wine she drinks being likened to their blood (Rev. 16:6; 1:7; 18:24). The cup, which is the measure of her sins becomes, fittingly, the measure of God's anger and judgment poured out against her (Rev. 14:10; 15:7; 16:1; 18:4-8). In fact, the judgment will be, "In the cup which she has mixed, mix twice as much for her" (Rev. 18:6).

Another Tabernacle Connection

Bowls or basins were used in the tabernacle and temple worship. According to the New Unger's Bible Dictionary, "A large bowl (Heb. Mizraq) was a part of the furnishing of the tabernacle and temple, particularly in service of the altar of burnt offering (Num. 4:14) to hold the grain offering and to receive sacrificial blood (Zech. 5:19; 14:20). It was commonly made of gold or silver. In inordinate revelling, wine is said to be drunk from such bowls (Amos 6:6). When Nebuchadnezzar, King of

Babylon, conquered Judah and sacked Jerusalem, he took some of these vessels with him back to Babylon and put them into the treasury of his god" (Dan.1:2).

Partying in Babylon

Belshazzar, a later king of Babylon, presided over its demise at the hands of the Persians. On the very night of the overthrow of the city of Babylon, Daniel 5 records that Belshazzar held a great feast for a thousand of his nobles, and the wine flowed freely. Then Belshazzar commanded his servant to bring the gold and silver vessels that had been taken from the house of God in Jerusalem. The king and his nobles drank from them, using them as cups. "They drank the wine and praised the gods of gold and silver, of bronze, iron, wood, and stone" (Dan. 5:4). It was then that the fingers of a man's hand wrote out a message from God on the palace wall, a message that spelled out the doom of Belshazzar and Babylon. It seemed that the desecration of the sacred vessels was the last act that filled up the measure of their guilt, and that very night the Medes and Persians overran the city. In like manner, the drinking of the cup by the Queen of Babylon is the last act of defiance against God that invites the outpouring of God's wrath in judgment. Could it be that today God's day of judgment is approaching?   Are we seeing the writing on the wall?

Seven Angels and Seven Bowls

Having seen the connection between the vessels in the temple and the judgment of Babylon of old, what happens next should be easily understood. Seven angels who have the seven plagues come out of the temple in heaven, and to them is given seven bowls full of the wrath of God (Rev. 15:5-7). It is reasonable to assume that these are the same angels who were involved with the trumpet judgments. There is an interesting reference in Numbers 31:6 where Moses sends out Phineas the priest with the army to do battle with the Midianites. He also sent "the holy vessels and the trumpets for the alarm in his hand." Now the vessels of the temple in heaven will be used by seven angels dressed in priestly clothes as vehicles of divine vengeance upon a world at war with God.

There is purposeful progression in the judgments of Revelation. The seal judgments, where the Lord allows man to practice his wickedness, brings destruction to a fourth of the earth. The trumpet judgments where God allows Satan to have his wicked way, results in destruction of one third of the earth. But the bowl judgments are the direct measure of God's wrath, and they result in ALL MEN being judged.

The Plagues of Egypt

The reference is often made to the similarity of these

judgments to the plagues of Egypt, and rightly so.

The first plague of malignant sores on men is like the sixth plague in Egypt. It is interesting to note that Moses initiated that plague by throwing handfuls of soot from a kiln into the air (Ex. 9:8–12).

The second and third plagues involve turning all the water in the world, both salt and fresh, into blood. It is this that causes the angel of the waters to laud the rightness of this judgment. "They poured out the blood of the saints and prophets, and Thou hast given them blood to drink. They deserve it"(Rev. 16:6).

The fourth angel pours his bowl out upon the sun, and the sun scorches the earth with fierce heat. I remember walking up to the hospital in the middle of an African heat wave at midday. The east wind blowing over the hot sand did not cool me, but rather blasted scorching air into my face, taking my breath away. That was hot! And there is much talk today about the greenhouse effect caused by pollution with the heating up of the planet. But when the final days of tribulation come, the whole world will experience heat as never before.

The fifth bowl is poured out upon the throne of the beast, throwing his kingdom into darkness, like the thick darkess that settled upon Egypt during the ninth plague

(Ex. 10:21-23). "But immediately after the tribulation of those days the sun will be darkened" (Matt. 24:29). It appears that the inky blackness will continue right up to the second coming of the Lord.

The sixth bowl brings the opening up of the eastern boundary of the promised land, the Euphrates River, so that the kings of the East with their vast armies will also be able to converge on the Middle East. Three unclean spirits, issuing from the mouths of the evil triumvirate, call the armies of the world to the battlefield. This is in sharp contrast to God's three angelic heralds at the beginning of this section (Rev. 14:6-13). The armies converge on Har-Magedon, which is often identified as the plain of Megiddo, a wide plain north of Jerusalem where notable battles were fought in the past. Included in those battles was Gideon's great victory over the Midianites. It is interesting to note that the story of Gideon begins with him in the winepress (Jud. 6:11), indicating the oppression of Israel, and ends with deliverance, and death of Zeeb, the Midianite king, in a winepress (Jud. 7:25). However, the name Har-Magedon itself means 'hill of the place of God' (Young's Concordance) and may be symbolic of the temple mount in Jerusalem, which is the center of attention in all this struggle.

The seventh bowl is a tremendous storm unequalled

in its ferocity, along with an earthquake "such as there has not been seen since man came upon the earth" (Rev. 16:18). Adding to the destruction is a hail-storm of epic proportions with hailstones weighing 100 lbs. each. This storm is worldwide in scale because it says, 'the cities of the nations fell" (Rev. 16:19), but the most concentrated destruction will fall on Babylon the Great, the seat of the beast. The speed of its destruction is emphasized by the little phrase, "in one hour' (Rev. 18:10, 17, 19). The coup de gras will be administered by fire.

Vision VI

CHRIST

THE KING OF KINGS

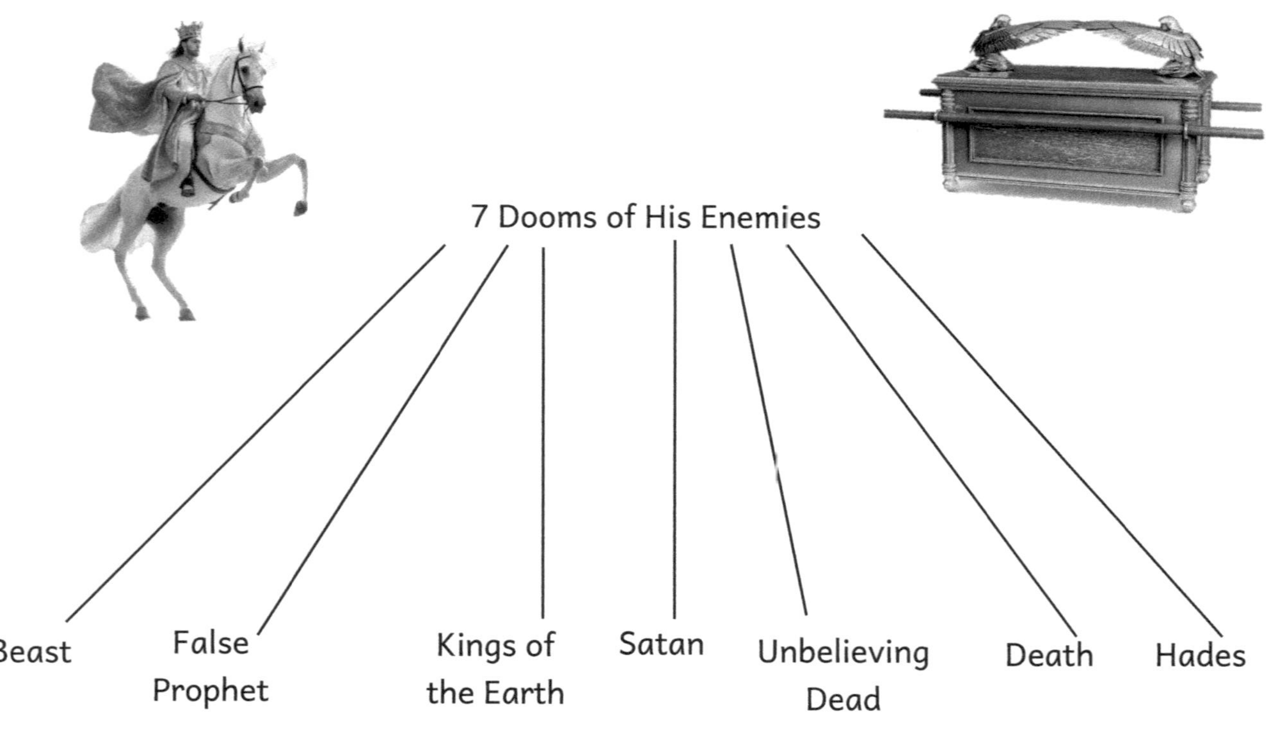

7 Dooms of His Enemies
Beast
False Prophet
Kings of the Earth
Satan
Unbelieving Dead
Death
Hades

Christ the King of Kings

Reminiscent of the dramatic change in venue in chapter 4:1, the scene of chapter 19 switches from earth to heaven, where, once again, a great praise gathering is taking place. As the faithful of Israel celebrated the Passover in Israel with Hallel Psalms, so the redeemed in heaven are now praising God with repeated hallelujahs for His great works. They first celebrate the righteous judgment of God upon Babylon, then they turn their attention to the preparations being made for a great marriage, the marriage of the Lamb. The bride is the church, and she has been making herself ready for her wedding day by the making of a fine linen garment, which is a symbol of her acts of righteousness. This symbolism is also expressed in Eph. 5:25-27 where the emphasis is upon Christ, the heavenly bridegroom, who is preparing His bride, the church, by sanctifying and cleansing her, to "present to Himself the church in all her glory, having no spot or wrinkle or any such thing; but that she should be holy and blameless". Hence, although the righteous acts of the bride are on display, the ultimate glory goes to Christ. The pure and holy bride contrasts with the evil prostitute which is Babylon.

When Kings Go Out to War

The action of the bowl judgments brought us up to the

point where all the mighty kings of the earth and their armies are gathered to Israel for the war of the great day of God, the Almighty. It is that final act of armed rebellion against God, and the resulting threat posed to the faithful remnant of Israel, that brings about the Second Coming of Christ (Zech. 14:1-3). As the door of heaven opened in chapter 4:1 to admit John (who represents the church) into heaven, so now the door is thrown open again (Rev. 19:11), and out pour the armies of heaven, angels and saints alike, with their King leading the attack.

Who is this King of Glory?

When He came the first time, only a few humble shepherds and magi from the East were made aware of His presence. When He comes again, "Every eye will see Him" (Rev. 1:7). How will He appear?

1. Sitting upon a white horse (Rev.19:11)

A rider upon a horse was, for centuries, a symbol of armed combat, and the white charger a symbol of the victor. A rider on a white horse has already appeared (Rev. 6:2), but as we have seen, his conquests result in death and hell. He is the great imposter. There is only one who is worthy and able to rule this world in righteousness and peace, and that is the Lord Jesus. "In righteousness

He judges and wages war." (Rev.19:11)

2. His eyes are a flame of fire (Rev.19:12)

Once before, as Head of the church, Jesus is described in this way. (Rev. 1:4). There His eyes are upon His own church, to love, judge and purify it. Now His fiery gaze is fixed on His enemies.

3. Upon His head are many diadems (Rev.19:12)

In Christ's appearance as a judge in chapter 14:14, He wears a golden crown on His head to remind us that this is a royal judge. This crown (Greek: stephanos) was much like the state crowns of monarchs today. Now we see Him crowned with many diadems (Greek: diadema). According to the New Unger Bible Dictionary, a diadem was a badge of royalty. "It was a band of silk, two inches broad, bound around the head and tied behind. Its colour was generally white, and it was sewn with pearl or other gems." The word diadem is found only in chapter 12:2 and 13:1, where the dragon and the beast are pictured wearing multiple diadems to denote their authority over many sovereign states. However, now comes their conqueror, the King of Kings. "The kingdom of the world has become the kingdom of our Lord and of His Christ; and He will reign forever and ever" (Rev. 11:15).

4. Clothed in a robe dipped in blood (Rev.19:13)

When Jesus came the first time, He wore no kingly garment, only the humble clothing of a carpenter. But, at His trial, after they had scourged Him, they dressed Him up in a purple robe, and put a crown of thorns on His head. In mockery they hailed Him as King of the Jews, as they alternately bowed to Him, then beat His head with a reed and spat on Him. The robe of purple must have been soaked through with the blood that oozed from His many wounds. Now all is changed. The royal robe is now thoroughly covered with blood, not His own blood, but that of His enemies, as He tramples them beneath His feet in the winepress (Is. 63:1-6; Rev. 14:19-20; 19:15).

5. From His mouth comes a sharp sword (Rev.19:15)

Concerning Messiah's coming, Isaiah declares, "Then a shoot will spring from the stem of Jesse and He will strike the earth with the rod of His mouth, and with the breath of His lips He will slay the wicked (Is. 11:1-5). The One who spoke the worlds into being will, with the same ease, deliver his enemies to judgment and doom. Then He will rule them with a rod of iron. The same one, who as a baby, was saved from the crushing rod of a satanically- inspired king (Rev.12:4-5), will now bear the sceptre of absolute authority, with none to oppose.

6. Four names of the King

On the heads of the beast, Satan's counterfeit king, are blasphemous names (Rev.13:1). By contrast, God's king bears four glorious names. Once again, these names remind us of the fourfold way the Saviour is presented in the gospels.

A. Faithful and True (19:11)

Luke presents to us a faithful and true account (Luke 1:1-4), of a faithful and true Saviour. In Luke, Jesus appears as the perfect man, who, by His life of faith and devotion, bears witness to the true and living God, and the faithfulness of his word (Luke 24:25-27). As this gospel opens with the story of Zacharias, the faithful priest, it closes with Jesus, as Son of Man, now qualified by His atoning death to be our priest, our Great High Priest, and bring us into a blessed fellowship with God (Luke 24:30, 47. 50-53).

B. The Word of God (19:13)

This name is found only in the writings of John. The apostle opens both his gospel and epistle with this title of the Lord. It emphasizes the deity of Christ, "The Word was God" (John 1:1). Other men speak God's word; Jesus is God speaking!

C. King of Kings and Lord of Lords (19:16)

Matthew opens with the genealogy of the King (son of David) and closes with the mandate of the King spoken from the mountain, "All authority has been given to me in heaven and on earth" (Matt. 28:18).

D. A name written upon Him that no one knows except Himself (19:17)

Secret names are usually names of love and endearment. In Mark's gospel, Jesus, as a servant of Jehovah, humbly does the Father's will, without thought of His own name or reputation. It was Christ's servanthood which prompts the Father to give Him a secret, glorious name, a "name above all names" (Phil. 2:4-10). It is thrilling to see that the faithful Christian, the one who bows to serve, will also receive a secret name from the Father (Rev. 2:17).

The Tabernacle Connection: the Ark

There was one item of furniture in the tabernacle, which, above all others, was associated with the presence of the King amid the camp of Israel, the ark of God. The ark was a wooden box, covered with gold, which rested in the Holy of Holies, the inner room of the tabernacle, behind the veil (Ex. 25:10-22).

Some years ago, Hollywood made a hit movie called "Raiders of the Lost Ark". The story line involved a search for the ancient ark during World War II, by both the Germans and the Americans, because they believed that whichever army possessed the ark would be successful in battle. Although the story is fictional, this part of the plot, at least, has a basis in fact.

The Ark a symbol of the Warring King

When the camp of Israel set out from Mt. Sinai, the ark was journeying in front of them. "Then it came about when the ark set out that Moses said, "Rise up, O Lord! And let thine enemies be scattered and let those who hate thee flee before Thee (Num. 10:35). When King Solomon dedicated the temple, he concluded his prayer of dedication with these stirring words; "Now therefore arise, O Lord God, to thy resting place, Thou and the ark of Thy might...(II Cor. 6:41). Both Moses and Solomon understood that this golden box was the symbol of the presence of the WARRING KING, the One who protected Israel by His great might!

Joshua meets the Captain

The ark led the way for Israel to enter Canaan by parting the waters of the Jordan River (Josh. 3:11). As Joshua, the leader of the army of Israel, pondered how to mount an attack against the strong walls of Jericho, he met the Captain of the Host of the Lord, the real leader of Israel, standing near him with a sword drawn (Josh. 5:13-15). He instructed Joshua in the Lord's battle plan, which featured the ark in prominent display as they circled the walls of Jericho. I believe the One who appeared to Joshua is the same Captain of the Host who, with drawn sword, will appear at that final battle of Armageddon. As we shall see, the ark, the symbol of the Warring king, will appear there also!

Dagon Decapitated

One day the Israelite armies lost a battle to the Philistines, and then decided to carry the ark with them into the battle so that they would be delivered from the power of their enemies (I Sam. 4:1-11). However, God allowed them to lose the battle because of the sins of the priests (I Sam. 2:32). The ark was taken by the Philistines, and placed in the temple of their god, Dagon, in Ashdod. Dagon was the fish god, with the head and arms of a man and the tail of a fish. The Philistines were a warrior tribe who admired human strength and ability more than anything, so Dagon, who represented all the power of natural resources, was a suitable god for them.

When the Ashdodites went in the next morning, Dagon had fallen on his face before the ark of the Lord, and they reverently returned him to his place. As if that was not enough to show them who the real God and King was, the following morning Dagon was not only on his face, but his head and hands were cut off (his feet were not cut off because he had none). Human resources are no match for divine power! In addition to the destruction of their idol, a deadly plague broke out in the city, so hurriedly they sent the ark back to Israel.

David's Delight

During the whole forty-year reign of King Saul, the ark is mentioned only once, when Saul once thought to bring the ark to the battlefield, but then changed his mind (I Sam. 11: 18-19). The proud and willful Saul did not honour the Captain of the Lord as the real King of Israel. But when David, the great warrior King of Israel, appears on the scene, the ark is brought from obscurity back into national prominence again. When the ark was carried into Jerusalem, David danced before it, clothed only in a simple linen garment. This incensed his wife, Michal, Saul's daughter, who sarcastically said, "How the King of Israel has distinguished himself today!" (II Sam. 6:20) David's reply showed his true heart, "It was before the Lord, who chose me above your father, and above all his house, to appoint me ruler over the people of the Lord, over Israel; therefore, I will celebrate before the Lord. And I will be more lightly esteemed than this and will be humble in my own eyes..." (II Sam. 6:21-22). David the King, was giving place to the King of Kings!

David's thoughts on this occasion are captured in Psalm 68, which begins with Moses' words as the ark would go out before the camp of Israel. Read the whole Psalm. It is not only a hymn of praise to the King, but a prophecy of the coming again of Jesus, the King of Kings, to Jerusalem from his heavenly sanctuary, when "He scatters the people who delight in war", and "rides upon the highest heavens".

The Psalm of the ark

Psalm 132 recounts the effort of David to bring the ark to Jerusalem. "Arise, O Lord, to thy resting place; Thou and the ark of thy strength" (Ps. 132:8). If the ark is a picture of the Warring king who comes to fulfill all His covenant with Israel, then the contents of the ark (Heb. 9:4) illustrate the blessings upon Israel when the ark returns again to its resting place, and the King sets up His Kingdom on earth (Rev. 20:4).

1. Material blessing	The golden jar of manna	Ps. 132:15
2. Righteousness	The tablet of the covenant	Ps. 132:9, 16
3. Authority for peace	Aaron's rod which budded	Ps. 132:17–18

The Ark in Revelation

It is beautiful to meditate on Jesus as the Warring King in Revelation 19, but where is the mention of the ark in this passage? It is plain that it is not expressly mentioned here. However, let us look at a passage that we only skimmed over before, one that takes place after the seventh trumpet blows. You will remember that, although Revelation is not strictly chronological, each section of the book is fairly chronological. The three series of judgments may not begin at the same time or advance at the same rate, but they come to the same endpoint. The sixth seal is the same time as the seventh trumpet, which is the same time as the seventh bowl. The action of Revelation 19 is after the seventh bowl, but it is happening at the same time as the aftermath of the seventh trumpet. What happens with the seventh trumpet is a celebration of the coming of the King (Rev. 11:15-19)! Verse 15 is a shout of victory. "The kingdom of the world has become the kingdom of our Lord, and his Christ; and he will reign forever and ever." Verse 17 and 18 is a prayer of thanksgiving by the church in heaven for the glorious events of the final battle, including the rage of the nations, the destruction of those who destroy the earth, the judging of the dead, and the rewards to God's people. But the statement of verse 19 is of paramount importance because the Ark appears.

The Ark Appears

Revelation 19:11 describes heaven breaking open to earthly view and the Warring King appearing. Revelation 11: 19 describes the opening of the temple of God in heaven and the ark of the covenant appearing. I believe that these are descriptions of the same event.

When the ark appears, there is a great storm which breaks out on the earth (Rev. 19:11). The lightning, and thunder and earthquake have all been seen before in Revelation as manifestations of Divine power, but the great hailstorm is mentioned only here and in the seventh bowl judgment (Rev. 16:21). They refer to one and the same hailstorm. Likewise, the celestial cataclysms of the sixth seal (Rev. 6:12-17) are part of the same storm.

The Seven Thunders

In Revelation 10, the seven thunders speak to John immediately after the Lord cries out with a loud voice, and then a voice from heaven intervenes and tells John not to write what the thunders utter.We still do not know what these seven thunders utter.We will know soon, for it says that when the seventh angel sounds the mystery of God will be finished (Rev. 10:7). All will be revealed then. For now, we are left to speculation.

Psalms 29 describes when the God of glory thunders. Seven times the thunder breaks forth as the Lord speaks, and a cataclysmic storm shakes the world. It is the King of Kings who is speaking, for verse 10 says, "The Lord sat as King at the flood; yes, the Lord sits as King forever". The seven thunders are the devastating details of the storm of the seventh bowl. If this is the case, then there are four series of seven judgments in the book of Revelation, not just three: seven seals, seven trumpets, seven bowls, seven thunders. It is intriguing that in Leviticus 26, four series of sevenfold judgments are poured out on those who reject the covenant of grace (LEV. 26: 18, 21, 24, 28).

The Seven Dooms

1 and 2. The Beast and the False Prophet

Since chapter 6:2, when this imposter king rode out on a white horse to present himself to the world as its saviour, the whole world has been in awe of him. "Who is like the beast and who is able to wage war with him" (Rev. 13:4)? Not only is this one a great political force, but a religious one as well. The false prophet, who is his second in command and minister of religious affairs, deceives the world to believe that this beast is God. They build a great image of him in the temple in Jerusalem and there they worship him as God.

Nebuchadnezzar, the King of the first great Gentile world power made a similar image of himself in Babylon, and issued a decree that all who did not bow down and worship it would be thrown into a fiery furnace. When God's three servants who resisted such blasphemy were thrown into the furnace, God rescued them, and Nebuchadnezzar understood there was a God in heaven over him. But his heart was still proud, and when he boasted about all his kingdom and power, God made him insane. He roamed the fields eating grass as an animal for seven years, until he finally acknowledged the sovereignty of God with these words, "Now I, Nebuchadnezzar, praise, exalt, and honour the King of heaven , for all His works are true and His ways just, and He is able to humble those who walk in pride." (Dan.4:37). Nebuchadnezzar repented, but not these two devil-inspired leaders of the last Gentile world power. They are thrown alive into the lake of fire which burns with brimstone (Rev. 9:20-21), and they become the first two occupants of the lake of fire.

3. The kings of the Earth

Why are the nations in an uproar, and the peoples devising a vain thing? The kings of the earth take their stand, and the rulers take council together against the Lord and against His Anointed: "Let us tear their fetters apart and cast away their cords from us!" He who sits in the heavens laughs, the Lord scoffs at them. Then He will speak to them in His anger and terrify them in His fury: "But as for me, I have installed My King upon Zion, My holy mountain" (Is. 2:1-6).

No doubt, kings and their armies from all over the world will be represented at Armageddon. But it would seem that the two main protagonists are the kings of the West (the revived Roman Empire), and the kings of the East.

The kings of the West

The makeup of this military force under the beast is described in chapter seventeen. The woman, called Babylon, who we discussed in the last chapter, is seen sitting on a scarlet beast. She represents the religious power astride the political power, like the relationship between Jezebel (religious) and Ahab (political) back in Israel's past. The beast has seven heads and ten horns. The heads represent successive kings who rule Babylon (Rev. 17:10). That five kings have fallen implies that they have passed into history already. One king is presently reigning, and another must also reign. At the time John was writing this, the Roman emperors were ruling the world. The Roman empire is symbolized by these seven kings. History records that the Roman empire came to an end. However, there is to be a revival of this as symbolized by the great vision of Daniel in chapter two of his book. Notice verse 40 which describes the fourth kingdom as the feet and toes of the image. The feet represent the old Roman Empire which eventually was divided into two, and then faded into history. The toes represent a revival of that empire in a coming day.

Notice in Daniel seven there is another vision of Daniel's which corresponds to the vision in chapter two, only this time the Gentile nations are no longer successive parts of the great image, but rather beasts. The fourth beast, Rome, has ten horns. These horns take on a life of their own and become ten political powers in their own right (Rev. 17:12). Over them is a ruler, the beast, represented by the little horn of Daniel chapter 7:8. He is also the eighth king as mentioned in Rev. 17:11.

It appears from all this that, in the last days, there will be a political, economic, and religious union of those countries that were once in the old Roman Empire. They will unite under the beast and become his power base for world domination. It is instructive to see that after the power has been consolidated in his hands, all vestige of religious ceremony and tradition is destroyed by these kings. They make war against the woman and burn her up with fire. (Rev.17:16) No trappings of religion are needed now. You just bow down and worship the beast, or else!

The Kings of the East

There has always been in history a great separation between East and West. Mighty nations of the East have come and gone without affecting life in the West very much, and the opposite is also true. With the dawn of the twentieth century and the coming of two world wars, that is no longer the case. The world is a global community and East and West are inextricably linked both economically and politically. What draws the kings of the East across the Euphrates River for the final contest with the Western armies, and ultimately with the Lord (Rev.16:12)? Could it be that they fear the West taking full control of the Middle East and its precious supplies of oil? Whatever draws them there, they nonetheless come, and the most populated nations of the world throw their greatest asset, human lives, into the fray.

Doom for the Kings

The battle is quickly over. Guided missiles, lasers, weapons, stealth bombers, and space age tanks are insufficient to resist the sword of the Lord (Rev. 19:21). After the holocaust of destruction, an angel calls to the birds of carrion to come and eat their remains at the great supper of God, a grizzly antithesis to the marriage supper of the Lamb.

The Zechariah Connection

The vision of Zechariah that corresponds to this part of Revelation is that of the four chariots (Zech. 6:1-8). A quote from Ryrie Study Bible summarized the action here. "A vision of God's judgment on the nations of the world, especially focusing on Babylon (the land of the north v. 8) which revolted three years later and was devastated and depopulated by the Persians (Zech 2:6-7). The vision may also depict the final subjugation of the world, especially 'Babylon', during the tribulation days (Rev. 11:15, 18:21)".

Zechariah pictures the activity of the angelic hosts in the final battle (Matt. 13:41). Notice the base from which they exit in verse 1, "from between the two mountains; and the mountains were bronze mountains."

David Baron, in his commentary on Zechariah, suggests that these bronze mountains are Mount Zion and Mount Olivet, because between these two mountains is the temple mount. This may be the case. My own impression is that these two mountains have not even been formed yet. In this same prophesy, Zech. 14:4-5, the Lord's feet will stand on the Mount of Olives, splitting the mountain from east to west, so that "half the mountain will move toward the north and the other half toward the south. And you will flee by the valley of My mountains." Why does the Lord specifically say, "My mountains?" It is because in the valley, between the two mountains, the judgment of the nations of the world will take place. Bronze speaks of judgment. The Lord's feet of burnished bronze (Zech. 1:15) will be planted on each side, and from that valley of destruction the angelic messengers of God will gather from the world all that defile and bring them to this same valley for judgment.

4. Satan

"In that day the Lord will punish Leviathan the fleeing serpent, with His fierce sword, great and mighty, even Leviathan the twisted serpent; and He will kill the dragon who lives in the sea" (Is. 27:1). Revelation makes it clear that behind all the rebellion of the nations and the malevolence of its kings is 'the serpent of old', Satan himself! It was he who offered the Lord Jesus the kingdoms of the world, (for they were his to offer), in

return for worship offered to him (Matt. 4:8-9). It was
he who was behind the evil genius of ancient Babylon.
Isaiah 13 and 14 describe the destruction of Babylon
and its king. The language of chapter fourteen expands
beyond limits of time and space to a great event in a past
eternity when a great one, called Lucifer, the star of the
morning, said, "I will ascend to heaven; I will raise my
throne above the stars of God...I will make myself like the
Most High". This was the original sin, the proud boast
of a created being that he could become God. Lucifer is
undoubtedly Satan.

The serpent deceived Eve with the same seductive lie,
"You shall be like God, knowing good and evil" (Gen.3:5).
He has deceived the nations of the world down through
history with the same Lie. From Nebuchadnezzar (Dan.
4:30) and Herod (Acts 12:21) to the present, The Lie has
caused the nations and its leaders to vaunt their glory
and power in rebellion against God. The beast and the
false prophet are both called to prominence by the dragon
(Rev. 13:1-11), and the worship of the beast becomes
the worship of the dragon who empowered him (Rev.
13:4). The receiving of the worship of mankind is Satan's
greatest attempt to dethrone the King of Kings and be
recognized as the supreme monarch.

Bound for a Thousand Years

When the King returns in triumph, Satan will be thrown

into the abyss, the prison for evil spirits, for one thousand years (Rev.20:3).. It is during this time that the earth will enjoy the fulfillment of all the scripture promises of an earthly reign of Christ with Israel as the premier nation of the world, and Jerusalem as its exalted capital (Is. 2:1-4; 60:1-22; Zeph. 3:9-20). The personal presence of the King will guarantee a world of righteousness, peace, and prosperity. Those who have suffered for Christ during the tribulation period along with the saints of other ages, will be rewarded with positions of authority and honour in the kingdom. "They will be priests of God and of Christ and will reign with Him for a thousand years" (Rev. 20:6).

Released for a Short Time

After this thousand years of utopian conditions on the earth, Satan will be released for a short period. We might question why this is necessary, but God has a reason. Perhaps it is to prove, once and for all, the justice of His sovereign acts. After experiencing the most amazing period of blessing this world has ever seen, there will still be many who will listen to Satan and rebel against the King. Man, although living in a perfect environment, still has an evil heart of unbelief, and when Satan's presence presents him with an alternative to worshipping the true God and Prince of Peace, he jumps at the chance. This rebellion will be worldwide and will generate a great army who presume to advance against Jerusalem. But they will be wiped out by fire from heaven (Rev. 20:9; Ez. 38:22).

Doomed to the Lake of Fire

Satan's days are numbered. At the end he will be thrown into the lake of fire, where eternal torment awaits (Rev. 20:10).

5. The Unbelieving Dead

"And I saw the dead, great and small, standing before the throne..." (Rev. 20:11).
It is the King who sits upon the throne, for all judgment has been committed to Him (John 5:22). Death and Hades are emptied of their occupants. All not previously raised are then raised to life again that they might physically be present at their trials. The books are the records of deeds done. There will be no argument for the defense, for the scripture declares that "every mouth will be closed and all the world will become accountable to God" (Ro. 3:19). These who have lived and rejected the Saviour will die the second death without a Saviour. "And if anyone's name was not found written in the book of life, he was thrown into the lake of fire" (Rev. 20:15).

6. Death

"For He must reign until He has put all enemies under His feet. The last enemy that will be abolished is death"

(I Cor. 15:26). When Adam sinned, the principle of corruption immediately came into effect for all men. Since that day, mankind has fought in vain against this last enemy. Full graveyards give silent witness to the failure of medical science to stop the aging process and cheat death of its victims. Only one has broken the bonds of death, the Lord Jesus. Now victorious over this enemy, He says, "I am alive forevermore, and I have the keys of death and Hades" (Rev. 1:18). Now death will be swallowed up in victory; death itself will die!

7. Hades

Together with death, Hades will be cast into the lake of fire. Hades (Sheol in the Old Testament) is the place of departed spirits, the unseen state which follows death. It might be compared to the local jail in which a criminal might be kept while awaiting sentencing. When sentence is passed, then he is shipped off to the penitentiary. Now emptied of its occupants, Hades serves no further purpose, and it too, is cast into the lake of fire.

Another Zechariah Connection

Following the visions of Zechariah, there is a scene which describes the crowning of Joshua, the high priest, beginning at chapter 6:9. That this is a symbolic act is obvious for the following reasons:
1. Priests were never crowned in Israel.
2. The crown belonged to the King only.

3. The offices of the priest and king were to be strictly
 separated. King Uzziah tried to usurp the office of priest
when one day he went into the Holy Place to offer incense
at the golden altar, but he was immediately judged by God
(II Chron. 26:16).
4. The symbolism is explained for us in Zech. 6: 12,13.
The man, whose name is Branch is the Messiah who will
rebuild the temple and will then rule as both Priest and
King. That the Branch will be the High Priest 'in that day',
the day of Messiah's kingdom, has already been stated in
Zechariah 3:8-10. Zechariah concludes his book with a
description of the rule of the King 'in that day'. "And the
Lord will be King over all the earth; in that day the Lord
will be the only One, and His name the only One" (Zech.
14:9).

The answer to all of this in Revelation is the one-
thousand-year reign of Christ on the earth. The Warring
King will be crowned, and will become the Reigning
King. In fulfillment of all the Old Testament promises of
kingdom blessing, Christ will rule the nations with a rod
of iron. All the faithful of the tribulation period and the
believers of the church period will rule with Him (Rev.
20:4; 2:26-27). Then it will come about that any who are
left of all the nations that went against Jerusalem will
go up from year to year to worship the King, the Lord of
Hosts (Zech. 14:16).

Vision VII

CHRIST IMMANUEL

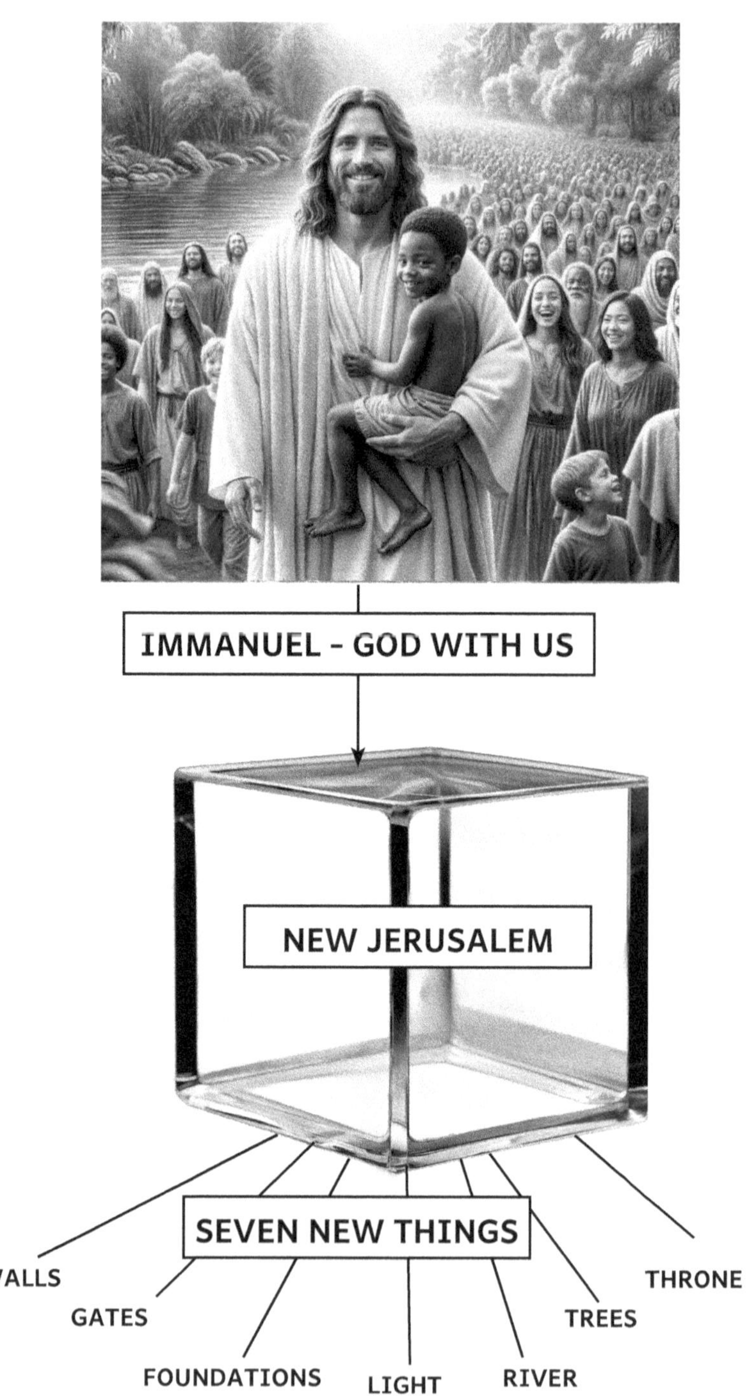

IMMANUEL - GOD WITH US
NEW JERUSALEM
SEVEN NEW THINGS
WALLS
GATES
FOUNDATIONS
LIGHT
RIVER
TREES
THRONE

Christ Immanuel

Seven is the number of perfection, especially spiritual perfection. In the last two chapters of Revelation we come to the seventh picture of Christ, the One which completes the whole, bringing it to spiritual perfection.

What could be added to the six magnificent titles of Jesus that he bears thus far; Head of the Church, Saviour of the World, Great High Priest, Great Prophet of our God, Judge of All, King of kings? Of all these titles this is the most awesome, it is God himself! He is spiritual perfection, "God Himself shall be among them" (Rev. 21:3). Here is Immanuel, which means "God with us", the one of whom John said, "And the Word became flesh and dwelt (tabernacled) among us and we beheld His glory, glory of the only begotten from the Father, full of grace and truth (John 1:14). "No man has seen God at any time; the only begotten God, who is in the bosom of the Father, He has explained Him" (John 1:18).

He Who Sits on the Throne

I believe the One sitting on the throne is none other than the Lord Jesus. Let us look at the details in order to affirm this: first what He says, and then, what He does.

What He says

1. "Behold I am making all things new." (Rev.21:5)

These are the words of the Creator. It is said of Jesus, "All things came into being by Him, and apart from Him nothing came into being that has come into being" (John 1:3) Time and again He demonstrated his creative power. John records how He opened the eyes of a man born blind. He did it by spitting on the ground, making clay of the spittle, and applying the clay to the man's eyes (John 9:6). This symbolizes the initial act of man's creation when God formed man out of the dust of the ground. Making things new is also Christ's genius in the spiritual realm. "If any man is in Christ, he is a new creature; old things have passed away; behold, new things have come (II Cor. 5:7). In the same way, as Isaiah predicted, the Lord will create new heavens and a new earth
(Is. 65:17, 6:22; Matt. 24:35, II Pet. 3:1-13).

2. "Write, for these words are faithful and true."

The same order to write was issued by Christ to John in the beginning of Revelation (1:11). Christ said concerning His own words of prophecy, "Truly I say to you, this generation will not pass until all these things take place.

Heaven and earth shall pass away, but My words shall not pass away" (Matt. 24:34-35). As we saw already, His very name is faithful and true (Rev. 19:11).

3. "It is done."

This reminds us of the great cry of Christ from the cross when He said, "It is finished" (John 19:30). What He had finished was the work of purchasing our redemption. A similar cry is heard out of the temple from the throne at the beginning of the seventh bowl judgment (Rev. 16:17). It is the voice of the Judge-King declaring the final act of judgment upon the earth. Again here, as the creative act of establishing a new heaven and earth culminates in the descent of New Jerusalem from heaven, the Lord Jesus exclaims, "It is done!"

4. "I am the Alpha and the Omega, the beginning and the end."

In Rev.1:8, it is the Lord God who applies this name to Himself. But in Rev. 22:13, it is obviously Jesus who calls Himself by that name. Alpha is the first letter of the Greek alphabet and Omega is the last. The implication is that Jesus is indeed the Lord God, God, the origin of all intelligence and language. the One who is the author and finisher of all things (Heb. 12:2).

5. "I will give to the one who thirsts from the spring of water of life without cost."

The words of Jesus speaking to the woman at the well immediately come to mind, "Whoever drinks of the water I shall give him shall never thirst, but the water that I shall give shall become in him a well of water springing up to eternal life" (John 4:14).

6. He says, "He who overcomes shall inherit these things, and I will be his God and he will be my son."

These words are comparable with the words of Christ to the overcomer of the church of Laodicea in Rev. 3:21. The testimony of Thomas when he realized he was in the company of the overcoming Christ was, "My Lord and my God" (John 20:28).

7. He says, "But for the cowardly and unbelieving and abominable and murderers and immoral persons and sorcerers and idolators and all liars, their part will be in the lake that burns with fire and brimstone, which is the second death."

It is sobering and instructive to observe that Jesus spoke
of hell more than he spoke of heaven. Now the Judge-
King is pronouncing the final verdict which is eternal
banishment from the presence of God.

What He Does

"He shall wipe away every tear from their eyes". He
who was called the man of sorrows, who Himself wept in
sorrow (John 11:35) and in agony (Luke 22:44) and spent
Himself bearing others griefs, will now culminate His
ministry by comforting all who mourn. Human hands will
wipe away human tears (Heb. 2:18; Is. 25:8), the curse
will be lifted (Gen. 2:17; Rev. 22:3), and then death and
mourning and crying and pain will be forever done away.

The Tabernacle Connection: The Mercy Seat

The mercy seat was the golden lid of the ark of the
covenant. Rising from the golden base were two golden
cherubim whose wings touched one another and whose
faces were turned in to overlook the ark. Of all the pieces
of furniture in the tabernacle, the mercy seat was the one
identified with the immediate presence of God. God told
Moses, "And there I will speak to you about all that I will
give you in commandment for the sons of Israel" (Ex. 25:22).

The only day in all the year that anyone from Israel actually saw the mercy seat was on the Day of Atonement. The mercy seat in the Holy of Holies was separated from the Holy Place by a veil. To pass through the veil meant death to the intruder, unless it was only the high priest, and only on the Day of Atonement, and only with the blood of a sacrificed animal. The blood was then sprinkled seven times on the mercy seat. Leviticus 16 describes all the details, but it is summarized in Hebrews 9.

All this is a picture of the day when our Great High Priest, the Lord Jesus, went to the cross of Calvary. There He became the sin offering for us (Is. 53:10; II Cor. 5:21). On the basis of His finished work, He then entered the heavenly sanctuary, not the temple in Jerusalem, having obtained eternal redemption for us.

The mercy seat is therefore aptly named. It is the place where mankind finds mercy and forgiveness where once was death and judgment. The word for mercy seat in Hebrew is "kapporeth", meaning "cover". The ark, which contained the law which judged without mercy, now is covered by a blood-stained seat of mercy. Mercy triumphs over judgment (James 2:13)!

The word for mercy seat in Greek is "hilasterion". It is also translated 'propitiation", which means "that which allows God to be merciful". This word is explained in Romans 3:25 where Jesus, by value of his sacrifice, is the propitiation for our sins. Again, in I John 2:2, it is Jesus who is the propitiation for our sins. Jesus is the hilasterion. Jesus is the mercy seat!

The Throne of Grace

Another name for the mercy seat is the throne of grace (Heb. 4:16). A throne speaks of kingly authority and rule (Ps. 99:1). The temple was not just the spiritual centre of Israel but also its political centre. It was not just a temple, but a residence for a king! And so it had a throne room (Holy of Holies) and a throne (the mercy seat)! When Isaiah had a vision of the Lord in glory he said, "I saw the Lord sitting on a throne, lofty and exalted, with the train of his robe filling the temple" (Is. 6:1).

The throne was in the temple.

The priests who served in the temple had nowhere to sit; they continually stood and served. However, the book of Hebrews describes the work of our great High Priest, who, when He had brought the blood of His sacrifice into the Holy of Holies, sat down at the right hand of the Majesty on high (Heb. 1:3). "Right hand" simply means the place of highest honour. Again, it says, "We have such a High

Priest who has taken His seat at the right hand of the throne of the Majesty in the heavens, a minister in the sanctuary" (Heb. 8:1-2). The question is, "Where does our High Priest sit?" He sits on the throne of God, the mercy seat, which is in the Holy of Holies. That is because He is not only priest, but King, and not only King, but King of Kings, and Immanuel, God Himself with us!

When we look at these closing verses in Revelation, we see a new name for the throne of God. It is "the throne of God and of the Lamb" (Rev. 22:1,3). However, this is even more strongly affirmed back in 7:17, where it says, "For the Lamb in the centre of the throne shall be their shepherd, and shall guide them to the springs of the water of life; and God shall wipe every tear from their eyes".

The Zechariah Connection

At the close of the last chapter, we referred to the symbolic crowning of Joshua found in Zech. 6:9-15. There the Lord Jesus is pictured as the Priest-King. In the dual role of Priest-King He will rule this world during the Millenium. His capital city will be Jerusalem (Zech. 14:17, Is. 24:23) and His throne will be the mercy seat (Ps.47:8). Zechariah makes no mistake in identifying the One who will come to be Priest-King. In chapter 14 he declares, "Then the Lord, my God, will come, and all the holy ones with Him." (Zech.14:5)

Recently I had a discussion with a Watchtower missionary at our door. When I stated my belief that Jesus was physically raised from the dead and that He would physically return to this world to reign as King, the man scoffed and said there was no need of all of this. "It is all to be spiritually interpreted", he said. I showed him the verses in Zechariah 14 using his own Bible and received an unexpected encouragement. In verse 4 of their "New World Translation" it says, "and in that day His feet will ACTUALLY stand on the Mount of Olives". Whose feet? The feet of the King of Kings. Whose feet? According to verse 5, the feet of the Lord, my God. May His name be praised!

The New Jerusalem

In verses 9 and 10 of chapter 21, one of the angels who carried one of the seven bowls of judgment, carries John away in the Spirit and shows him the holy city, the New Jerusalem, coming down out of heaven from God. This action parallels the activity of the beginning of chapter 17 where one of these same angels carries John in the Spirit into a wilderness and shows him the woman sitting on the scarlet beast, which represents Babylon. Thus, we are meant to contrast Babylon with the New Jerusalem.

The first city is called a harlot, the second one the bride of the Lamb. The first city is full of uncleanness. Into the second, no evil will ever enter (Rev. 21:27). The first city gorges itself on the wealth of the earth, bringing slavery and death to many (Rev. 18:13). The second city has a river of life which flows out to bless the world, and trees, the leaves of which are for the healing of the nations (Rev. 22:2). The occupants of the first city engage in occupation without any honoring of God (Rev. 18:22-24). The occupants of the second, as kings and priests, will reign with the Lord and serve Him forever (Rev. 22:3-5). The first city honours the beast, the antichrist, and worships him through witchcraft (Rev. 18:23). The second city honours the King of Kings (Rev. 21:22). The first city ends in a plague of darkness (Rev. 16:10). The second will enjoy the light of the glory of God forever (Rev. 21:2, 22:5). The first will end in a violent day of destruction (Rev. 18:21). The second will endure forever and forever (Rev.22:5).

The New Holy of Holies

There is one final reference to the tabernacle and temple in Revelation which brings the book to a fitting climax. It is this: the new Jerusalem is a new Holy of Holies! The Holy of Holies was the most sacred part of the temple, where the ark and the mercy seat were located. God dwelt in that enclosure, but the people did not. God was present in the middle of Israel but was none the less separated from His people. The blood of Christ described a path from the altar of sacrifice to the mercy seat and opened a way whereby we could draw near to God through the veil (Heb. 10:19-22). In the New Jerusalem, we draw near to God, never to part. There is no temple in the city simply because THE WHOLE CITY IS THE TEMPLE (Rev. 21:22). The Holy of Holies has grown to incorporate the whole of the city. The Holy of Holies serves as a prototype of the New Jerusalem, as illustrated in the diagram.

Consider these comparisons:

1. The Holy of Holies was a perfect cube (I Kings 6:20), so is the New Jerusalem (Rev. 21:16), only now it is of far greater dimensions, not just 20 cubits but 1500 miles!

2. The Holy of Holies in the temple was encased in gold (I Kings 6:20; II Chr. 3:8), so is New Jerusalem (Rev.21:18).

3. The Holy of Holies had a floor lined with gold (I Kings 6:22). In his book entitled "The Temple" Edersheim states that the temple was "built on immense foundations of solid blocks of white marble covered with gold". The streets of the New Jerusalem are gold (Rev. 21:21).

4.***The temple was decorated with many precious
stones*** (II Chr. 3:6). The New Jerusalem will have twelve
precious stones in its foundation, each representing one
of the twelve apostles (Rev. 21:19-20).

5.**The temple was lighted by Shekinah, the glory of
God's presence, which was represented by the glory
cloud** (Ex. 40:34-38; II Chr. 7:1-3).

The New Jerusalem needs no light of sun or moon to shine
upon it, for the glory of God has illuminated it, and its
lamp is the Lamb (Rev. 21:23). The whole structure of the
city is crystalline, even the gold is transparent, so that its
light will pass through it and light up heaven and earth!

6. **The Holy of Holies had a veil over its entrance on
which were embroidered cherubim** (Ex.36:35)

Similarly, angels guarded the entrance to Eden with a
flaming sword (Gen.3:24) to remind those who would
enter there of the penalty of illegal entry. In the temple of
Solomon, in addition to the embroidered angels in the veil,
there were angels carved into the golden walls (II Chr.
3:7). At the gates in New Jerusalem are stationed angels,
no doubt with the same symbolism in mind.

7. The Holy of Holies had a throne in the middle of it

This throne, as we have seen, was the mercy seat. Now the throne is in the middle of the New Jerusalem (Rev. 22:1-3).

Drawing Near in Hebrews

In Hebrews 4:16, we are invited to draw near with confidence to the throne of grace, where our Saviour-Priest is seated. Because Christ has now entered within the veil (Heb.10:19-20), we are again encouraged to draw near (inside the Holy of Holies). Finally in Heb. 12:22 it says, "You have come to Mount Zion and the city of the Living God, the heavenly Jerusalem. When we at last come to the heavenly Jerusalem, we will discover that the city of the Living God is the same place as the Holy of Holies and the throne of grace, for the throne of grace is in the Holy of Holies, and the Holy of Holies will become the New Jerusalem!

Seven New Things for a New City

Jesus said, "Behold, I am making all things new" (Rev.21:5). There are seven new things described in the new city of Jerusalem.

1. New Walls

Ancient cities were vulnerable to attack from hostile armies if they did not have strong defence that included a thick and high wall encircling the city. Old Jerusalem was a walled city. The mission of Nehemiah was to rebuild the walls after they had been breached and broken by Babylonian siege. Today, various parts of the old walls have been exposed in archeological diggings.

What are the walls of New Jerusalem like? "It had a great and high wall with twelve gates and he measured its wall, 72 yards according to human measurements, which are also angelic measurements, and the material of the wall was jasper; and the city was pure gold, like clear glass" (Rev. 21:11, 12,18). Just as the ancient walls meant security for the inhabitants of Jerusalem, so these new walls speak of ETERNAL SECURITY. Isaiah says, "You will call your walls salvation" (Is. 60:18).

One of the insecurities of this earth is that we live precariously on the thin outer skin of the planet, moving in a pocket of air called the atmosphere, preserved from deadly radiation only a millimeter's thin coating of ozone above that. In the New Jerusalem we will no longer live on, but in! The protective walls of the city will encircle us and enclose us in the secure atmosphere of God's eternal presence.

2. New Gates

"It had a great and high wall of twelve gates and at the gates twelve angels; and on them were written the twelve tribes of Israel...and the twelve gates were twelve pearls; each one of the gates was a single pearl...its gates shall never be closed...and they shall bring the glory and the honour of the nations into it, and nothing unclean and no one who practices abomination and lying shall ever come into it, but only those whose names are written in the Lamb's book of life (Rev. 22:12, 21, 24-27).

Although gates were part of the wall of the city and contributed to its security, they also were the channels of commerce and industry, where guards allowed in and out that which was good for the city, and disallowed that which was for ill. In the New Jerusalem, there were twelve gates, each guarded by an angel, so that nothing of evil will enter in; however, all that is of glory and honour will be allowed free entry. Isaiah says, "You will call... your gates PRAISE" (Is 60:18).

Again, the cry of the faithful is "to make Jerusalem a praise in the whole earth" (Is. 62:6-7). The name Judah means 'praise'. That was to be the occupation of the sons of Judah; they were meant to praise God. When the church, composed of Jew and Gentile in one body, is resident in the New Jerusalem, that will be our occupation as well. The gates will open wide to export the praises on the lips of God's redeemed to the far reaches of the new heaven and new earth. We will forever "proclaim the excellencies of Him who called you out of darkness into His marvelous light" (I Pet. 2:9).

3. New Foundations

"And the wall of the city had twelve foundation stones and on them were the names of the twelve apostles of the Lamb. The foundation stones of the city were adorned with every kind of precious stone" (Rev. 21:14,19). "Now these are the foundations which Solomon laid for building the house of God" (II Chr. 3:3). A good foundation guarantees permanence. Where we were working in Africa, many people lived in mud huts and built their homes on sand. When the rains came, the torrents of water would often sweep under the walls of these meagre dwellings and soon destroy them. The patriarch Abraham was not satisfied with the temporal nature of earthly foundations. "He was looking for a city which has foundations, whose architect and builder is God" (Heb. 11:10).

The church is "built upon the foundation of the apostles and prophets, Christ Jesus himself being the cornerstone" (Eph. 2:20). The foundation is not the men, but the message, the word of God. That is the sure foundation. Jesus said, "Heaven and earth will pass away, but My words shall not pass away" (Matt. 24:35). God's unchangeable word guarantees the permanence of the New Jerusalem.

4. A New River

"And he showed me a river of the water of life, clear as crystal, coming from the throne of God and the Lamb" (Rev. 22:1). "Now a river flowed out of Eden to water the garden and from it divided and became four rivers" (Gen. 2:10).

The area around Kalene Hospital in Zambia where we lived is a watershed. It is on the high central ridge of Southern Africa. A few miles to the south the mighty Zambezi River finds its origin in a secluded rain forest, and flows to the Indian ocean. A few miles to the east the great Congo River begins its journey to the Atlantic. These rivers owe their birth to the abundant rain on this lush fertile highland. The garden of Eden was just such a highland with first one river flowing out of it, then four rivers branching off to flow in different directions.

In the Millenium, the temple of Jerusalem will be situated on just such a highland. God will change the topography of the land so that Jerusalem will rise to become a greater height than at present, and the land around it will become a plain (Zech. 14:10). These changes, plus the splitting of the Mount of Olives to the east, will prepare the area for a river flowing from beneath the temple in Jerusalem (Ez. 47:1-2). The river will quickly divide and flow east and west, bringing fresh, lifegiving water to a polluted and dying world (Zech. 14:8).

In the New Jerusalem, there is a river flowing out from the throne, and then down from the heights of Zion to bring life to all the inhabitants of that country. The Lord Jesus explained what this river was when one day He stood in the middle of Jerusalem and cried, "He who believes in me, as the scriptures said, from his innermost being shall flow rivers of living water" (John 7:38).

The next verse states that this flowing river is the Holy Spirit that comes from God. The blessed third person of the Trinity will be there in New Jerusalem providing an unending draught of eternal life (Rev. 21:6).

5. New Trees

"And on either side of the river was the tree of life, bearing twelve kinds of fruit, yielding its fruit every month; and the leaves of the tree were for the healing of the nations" (Rev. 22:2).

There was a tree of life in the garden of Eden, whose fruit provided life for Adam and Eve. Ezekiel describes how the barren wilderness of the slopes east of Jerusalem, heading down to the Dead Sea, will be turned into verdant forest by the river (Ez. 47:7). From there, wherever the river goes it will bring life and renew the earth.

Ecologists today warn us that we are perilously near the point of no return for the destruction of our environment. Nothing short of a miracle, they say, will save our planet. Here is the miracle! A lifegiving river and then, beautiful new trees to replenish the earth once again.

In the New Jerusalem, it will be even more beautiful than nature's best on earth. Every month their branches will groan with a fresh harvest of delicious fruits, and their leaves will have marvelous medicinal powers.

The Scriptures leave us in no doubt what these trees represent. "The fruit of the righteous is a tree of life" (Prov. 11:30). "And he will be like a tree firmly planted by streams of water which yields its fruit in its season" (Ps. 1:3). "So, they will be called oaks of righteousness, planting of the Lord, that He may be glorified" (Is. 61:3). The first tree in the garden was a picture of the Righteous One, Jesus. Those in heaven who bear His likeness are trees of life also. They are people of God, not only enjoying the living waters of heavenly bliss, but gainfully employed and bountifully productive in the service of the king. "And His bondservants shall serve Him" (Rev. 22:3).

6. The New Throne

"And the throne of God and of the Lamb shall be in it" (Rev. 22:3). All the other new things in heaven, glorious though they may be, pale when the throne comes into view. Isaiah, Ezekiel, Stephen and Paul all saw this glorious sight. Isaiah said, "Woe is me, for I am ruined! For my eyes have seen the King, the Lord of Hosts!" (Is. 6:5). Ezekiel fell on his face in fear and amazement (Ez. 1:28). Stephen's face was radiant with the fullness of the Spirit (Acts 7:55-56).. Paul, the man of words, simply said, "Inexpressible" (II Cor. 12:4). But we will see a new throne, new because it includes us. We will

gather round and sit there with the beautiful Lamb of
God, see His face, hear His voice, feel His touch, and
know that we are His and He is ours, forever.

7. New Light

"And the city has no need of the sun or of the moon to
shine upon it, for the glory of God has illuminated it,
and its lamp is the Lamb. And the nations shall walk by
its light...and there shall no longer be any night; they
shall not have need of the light of a lamp nor the light
of the sun, because the Lord God shall illumine them"
(Rev. 21:23-24; 22:5). God said, "Let there be light";
and there was light" (Gen. 1:3). Since that day of first
creation, we on this planet have depended on natural
light for sight, and warmth, and life itself. In time, man
discovered how to produce artificial light, a candle
or a lamp. None of this will be of any use in the new
Jerusalem, because natural and artificial light will be
superseded by the supernatural light of heaven. What a
picture!

God is light. But where is this light emanating from?
Its lamp is the Lamb! That's because the light of the
knowledge of the glory of God will forever be in the face
of Jesus Christ (II Cor. 4:5).

He is the light of heaven! As that light has shined in our hearts, so it will shine through the crystal halls of heaven, out through the gold embossed transparent walls, and out to the far reaches of the new heavens and the new earth.

Picture, if you will, a light bulb, not a little one, but one 1500 miles wide, composed of a transparent golden shell, a ball of radiant energy. As you look closer, you will discern its nucleus, an arc of blazing whiteness, amazing to behold. Such will be the Lamb in the midst of the throne. And we, inhabitants of that rarified atmosphere of heaven, will shine with Him as the sun in the kingdom of our Father (Matt. 13:43).

THE HOLY OF HOLIES

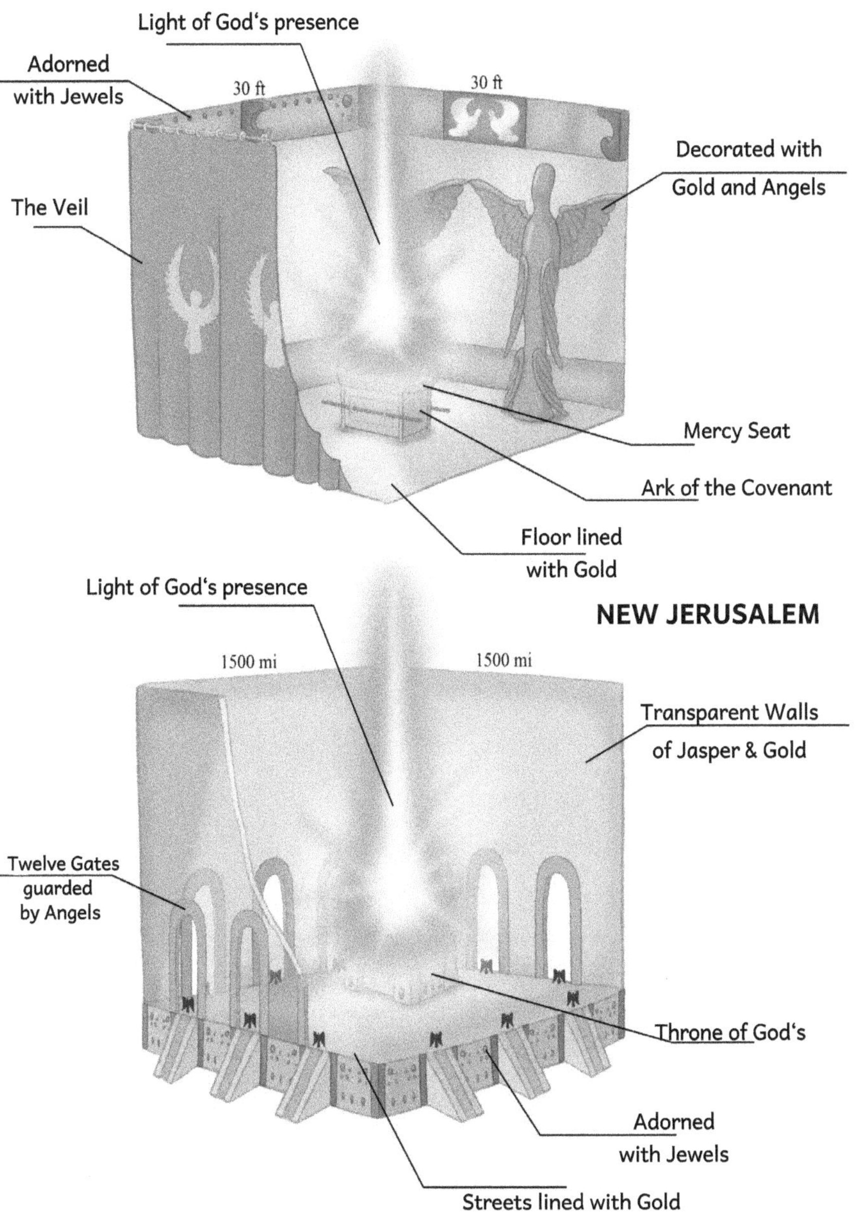

Epilogue: Rev.22:6-21

We have come to the end of this wonderful book of Revelation. As the last book in the Bible, these words convey to us God's final message.   Last words are very important, so we ought to pay special attention.   I see seven main thoughts in this passage.

1.Jesus wants us to know He personally sent this message. Vs.6, 16, 20

Three times Jesus speaks of how He personally has initiated this communication to us. Jesus himself testifies to these things. How precious is this great message of His love and care for us!

2.Jesus wants us to know there is a blessing for paying attention to Him. Vs. 7, 12,14, 21

In chapter 1:3, he pronounces a similar blessing for those who read, heed and take this prophecy to heart.   Now He holds out a blessing for those who consistently keep the words of the prophecy and diligently apply these teachings to life. Jesus calls for faith and obedience. He will reward those who heed.

3.Jesus wants us to remember who He is. Vs. 13,16

All through this book the emphasis is on seeing Jesus in all

His glory.   His glorious titles reflect His greatness. The Alpha and Omega, the First and the Last, the Beginning and the End; these names all speak of His deity.

Terms such as Root and Offspring of David, and the bright Morning Star bring out His humanity. Philippians 2:15-16 declares God's children shall all shine like the stars, but Jesus will shine the brightest by far. Truly, He is the altogether lovely One!

4.Jesus warns us to guard the message with all diligence. Vs. 7-10, 18-19

We guard the message in four ways.

First, don't confuse the message.   We may become confused like John and worship the lesser being, the angel, instead of the Lord himself. The angel corrected John. "Worship God alone!"

Second, don't hide the message. Don't seal it up because the Lord is coming soon and the time to declare it is now.

Third, don't add to the message and thus pollute it. It must remain pure.

Lastly, don't subtract from the message. Sometimes we think it best to leave out the difficult or unpleasant parts. Don't do it. Declare the whole counsel of God.

5.Jesus reminds us that there are only two final destinies, so choose wisely. Vs. 11, 14-15, 17

At the end, there are only two locations for the soul to reside, in the eternal city or forever banished from its precincts.   Make the wise choice and trust the Lord today.

6.Jesus wants us to know He is coming soon.Vs. 6-7

Three times he calls out and announces this message to his people. Two thousand years have passed since Jesus made this promise, but, compared to eternity, this time is short.   At the right time, He will return just as surely as He came the first time.

7.Jesus wants us to long for His coming. Vs.17, 21

Some people despair of his promise to return and become cold towards God and Christ.   If that is the state of your own heart, then let this book of Revelation revive your spirit. Our salvation is nearer than when we first believed. Christ waits at the door! In II Tim. 4:7-8,   the Apostle Paul confesses that he has fought the good faith, finished the course and kept the faith. He then encourages all of us as he anticipates receiving a crown of righteousness. That same crown awaits those who long for Christ's appearing.

The Spirit cries out
"Come".
Let that be the heart cry
of the bride as well.

So together we say,
"Come, Lord Jesus!"

Amen.